Learning Not to Fear the Old Testament

Learning Not to Fear the Old Testament

Word of His Mouth Publishers
Mooresboro, NC

All Scripture quotations are taken from the **King James Version** of the Bible.

ISBN: 978-1-941039-02-1
Printed in the United States of America
©2018 Dr. Bo Wagner

Word of His Mouth Publishers
Mooresboro, NC
www.wordofhismouth.com

Cover art by Chip Nuhrah

Table of Contents

Introduction

The Old Testament has become a weapon used by skeptics to tear down the faith of Christians. Here are just a few of the untrue things I have heard or read through the years:

"Your God promoted slavery like some plantation owner!"

"Your God allowed parents to sell their kids as sex slaves!"

"Your God said it was acceptable to murder children!"

"Your God said that if you ever wore clothes of mixed fabrics, you would go to hell!"

"Your God all through the Old Testament was all about hate!"

Christians rightfully spend most of their time in the New Testament, since it is our rule of faith and practice. But because of this, most Christians do not know how to answer when these things come up. Even when Christians do go to the Old Testament it is usually to the familiar and famous passages and people; Daniel, Noah, David, and the like. But the skeptic is going to go through the fine print, the legalese, and say a great many things about God that are not true or are intentionally twisted so as to denigrate His character.

Notice what Paul said:

Romans 15:1 *We then that are strong ought to bear the infirmities of the weak, and not to please ourselves.* **2** *Let* *every one of us please his neighbour for his good to edification.* **3** *For even Christ pleased not himself; but, as it is written, The reproaches of them that reproached thee fell on me.* **4** *For whatsoever things were written aforetime were written for our learning, that we through patience and comfort of the scriptures might have hope.*

In verses one and two, Paul was teaching us that we ought to sacrifice ourselves for the good of others. As an illustration of that, he reminded the readers that Christ Himself lived that way. And he then quoted a verse about Jesus, *The reproaches of them that reproached thee fell on me.* But Paul knew that verse about Christ was going to raise a bunch of questions in the minds of his readers because it was not from the New Testament, it was from the Old Testament:

Psalm 69:9 *For the zeal of thine house hath eaten me up; and the reproaches of them that reproached thee are fallen upon me.*

That verse was written 1,000 years before Christ. So, after he quoted that verse and applied it to Christ, Paul said, *For whatsoever things were written aforetime* (in the Old Testament) *were written for our learning, that we through patience and comfort of the scriptures might have hope.* All of the Old Testament was written down for us as a teaching tool. Here is the way Paul pictured it to the Galatians:

Galatians 3:24 *Wherefore the law was our schoolmaster to bring us unto Christ, that we might be justified by faith.* **25** *But after that faith is come, we are no longer under a schoolmaster.*

When the Old Testament is viewed in the way that God expects us to view it, we will not need to fear it. Paul said that it was written for our learning. That is why I have titled this book Learning not to Fear the Old Testament. We do not live under the law, we do not exist in the time of the Old Testament, but we do not need to fear the law or the Old Testament either. When we study it, we will find that what the scoffers have to say about it bears little to no resemblance to reality. My hope for this book, thus, is twofold. I would like for you to be able to withstand attacks by the scoffers and even to win them over with the truth. But more importantly to me, I would like this book to serve as a help for the Christian who is honest enough to admit that certain things in the Old Testament make him or her uncomfortable. There is no need to feel embarrassed over that... but there is also no reason to stay like that! When you are done studying this book, I believe you will never again fear the Old Testament.

And now, may I ask a favor of you, the reader? I am honest enough to admit that there are others far more skilled than I in the field of apologetics. But I also know that there is a great deal of collective wisdom and knowledge among God's people. If, as you are reading this book, you believe that I have gotten anything wrong, or perhaps omitted some necessary fact, would you please let me know? In so doing, future editions of this book may become better and better and better.

Thank you!
Pastor Bo Wagner

Chapter One
The Law of Mixed Fabrics

Leviticus 19:19 *Ye shall keep my statutes. Thou shalt not let thy cattle gender with a diverse kind: thou shalt not sow thy field with mingled seed: neither shall a garment mingled of linen and woollen come upon thee.*

Deuteronomy 22:9 *Thou shalt not sow thy vineyard with divers seeds: lest the fruit of thy seed which thou hast sown, and the fruit of thy vineyard, be defiled.* **10** *Thou shalt not plow with an ox and an ass together.* **11** *Thou shalt not wear a garment of divers sorts, as of woollen and linen together.*

You spouses, wherever you are, could you please examine the clothing tags and labels of your spouse (those you can reach modestly!) and tell us how badly you are all violating these two Old Testament passages?

Pretty badly, I'll bet! Because of that, in all of our churches, we are going to vote to change the church constitution. From now on, we not only pledge to abstain from alcohol, fornication, etc., but we will also all only wear clothing made of a single fabric. Cotton socks, wool underwear, polyester pants.

What in the world! The God of the universe, the sustainer of all life, the director of planetary systems, taking time to instruct men against wearing clothes of mixed fabrics? And here we are all disobeying it. What in the world do these verses mean? Why do we not follow them? Does this command mean anything for us today?

The context

To begin with, let me make you aware of the fact that these are the only two places in the Bible that this is mentioned. That is incredibly significant and let me tell you why; there is an argument that is constantly used by people to justify their wickedness of choice, and it is simply not true. But the fact that people have run around saying it for so long makes many people believe it is true. Here is the argument:

"Well, if you are going to believe that sodomy and lesbianism is an abomination just because the Old Testament says so, what are you going to do about your own abomination because the Old Testament also says that wearing mixed fabrics is an abomination, and all of you do that!"

There is just one problem with that: it is not true. Look at those two passages again and notice what word is not there. The word abomination. Anyone who tries to equate those two completely different things is being dishonest!

By the way, they are dishonest about all of the rest of the list I gave you at the outset as well. Here is an example:

Leviticus 19:29 *Do not prostitute thy daughter, to cause her to be a whore; lest the land fall to whoredom, and the land become full of wickedness.*

I mentioned a few paragraphs ago people claiming that God allowed His people to sell their daughters as sex slaves. Once again, the only problem is, it is one hundred percent not true.

But back to the mixed fabrics, we still need to deal with this and learn from it.

Every verse of the Bible is in a setting of some kind. There are other things around it or other verses in other places that help to round out the truth. *Always study Scripture in the light of its context!*

In Leviticus 19:19, before God mentioned the prohibition of mixed fabrics, He told them that they were also not to let cattle breed with different kinds and not to sow their fields with more than one kind of seed. In Deuteronomy, He told them not to mix seeds and not to plow with different kinds of animals yoked together. God never did mention the mixture of fabrics all by itself; every time He mentioned it, He lumped a lot of smaller things together to teach a greater truth, *the necessity of separation.* More about that later.

The consequences

In Deuteronomy 22:9, we find out that there are natural and negative consequences for disobedience in these areas:

Deuteronomy 22:9 *Thou shalt not sow thy vineyard with divers seeds: lest the fruit of thy seed which thou hast sown, and the fruit of thy vineyard, be defiled.*

When different kinds of seeds, plants, or trees are put together, there is a great tendency for them to become diseased, weak, and inferior. An apple tree is not supposed to be planted within *one mile* of a cedar tree, because of Cedar Apple Rust Disease!

Take a look at this instruction from a well-known gardening site:

> Potatoes and tomatoes ...do not grow well together. Do not plant these two crops next to one another because the presence of the tomato plant lowers the potato plant's individual resistance to Phytophthora infestants, commonly known as blight. This disease affects both tomato and potato plants. Once a plant is infected, blight spreads quickly from one plant to another, and even to other gardens close by. It can wipe out entire fields and was the cause of the Irish potato famine in 1845. (Richardson)

One million people died in that famine, and between that and people fleeing the country, the population of Ireland decreased by twenty-five percent.

When certain different grains are planted together, they disease each other, the ground, and the men and animals that eat them. More about that later, also.

The calling out

Not only were there natural consequences that compelled God to command this separation in all of these areas that He lumped together, but there was also a spiritual reason very relevant to Israel and all who loved God. The mixing of seeds affected physical health, but the mixture of fabrics was a danger to spiritual health. The pagan nations around them believed and taught that the mixing of seeds and fabrics gave them special favor with their false gods, and they would use these mixtures in their worship. (British Family Bible Notes, Leviticus 19:19) By commanding that God's people not wear these mixed fabrics, He was not trying to keep them healthy, He was commanding that they be visibly separate from the pagan world around them. No wonder these people were called the "church in the wilderness:"

Acts 7:38 *This is he, that was in the church in the wilderness with the angel which spake to him in the mount Sina, and with our fathers: who received the lively oracles to give unto us:*

They were not a *New Testament* church, but they were a church by separation. The word ekklesia (church) means a "called out assembly." God expected them to be separate and distinct from the world and that was His reasoning for the law of mixed fabrics. That law is not repeated for us in the New Testament, but things like the prohibition against sodomy and lesbianism are in places like Romans 1:26-28. It was part of the civil judicial law, not the moral law, whereas sexual prohibitions were part of the moral law, and all of those still apply even if not specifically mentioned in the New

Testament. Willmington noted the threefold division of the law as Moral, Spiritual, and Social. (1:71) Thomas Aquinas breaks them down into moral, ceremonial, and judicial:

> We must therefore distinguish three kinds of precepts in the old law; viz. "Moral precepts, which are dictated by the natural law: "ceremonial" precepts, which are determinations of the Divine worship: and "judicial" precepts, which are determinations of the justice to be maintained among men" (2a, Q99, A4)

But though we are not under the judicial law, the things we learn from it do apply today.

The conclusion

Again, the New Testament does not command that we, the church, wear garments of only one fabric. But the fact that the Old Testament commanded it for the Jews means that there is something we can learn from it. God was teaching that His people must be separate and that if we are not, we will become defiled and weak and produce poor fruit if any. Here is how the New Testament puts it:

2 Corinthians 6:14 *Be ye not unequally yoked together with unbelievers: for what fellowship hath righteousness with unrighteousness? and what communion hath light with darkness?*

We find in this passage that the New Testament equivalent of the Old Testament law of mixed fabrics is that we are not to unequally yoke with unbelievers. Here is another one just a few verses later:

2 Corinthians 6:17 *Wherefore come out from among them, and be ye separate, saith the Lord, and touch not the unclean thing; and I will receive you,* **18** *And will be a Father unto you, and ye shall be my sons and daughters, saith the Lord Almighty.*

In these two verses, we find that the New Testament equivalent of the Old Testament law of mixed fabrics is also that we are not to be partakers in uncleanness. The text says not to "touch" it. That means we are not only to not drink, not do drugs, etc., but we are not even to be near them. Whatever the sin is, we are not to be there when it happens, for our testimony will suffer "guilt by association." Here is another passage to consider:

2 Thessalonians 3:6 *Now we command you, brethren, in the name of our Lord Jesus Christ, that ye withdraw yourselves from every brother that walketh disorderly, and not after the tradition which he received of us.*

We find here that the New Testament equivalent of the Old Testament law of mixed fabrics is also that we are to withdraw ourselves from *brothers* who walk disorderly. Reading the context of that verse will tell you what Paul had in mind, laziness, but the principle itself goes much farther. If a Christian is living like a heathen, he is not to have the pleasure of our company while he is doing it! Here is yet another passage to see in light of all this:

1 Timothy 6:5 *Perverse disputings of men of corrupt minds, and destitute of the truth, supposing that gain is godliness: from such withdraw thyself.*

In this verse, we find that the New Testament equivalent of the Old Testament law of mixed fabrics is also that we are to be separate from those who are causing disputes contrary to the truth.

When God grabs our lapel and looks at our tags, He is not looking for a fabric content. He is looking for the tag on our heart that says "one hundred percent Biblical purity." We should not be looking for a fight, we should never be rude (And how twisted is it that, in some otherwise solid circles, rudeness has somehow become equated with holiness!), but as we draw closer to Christ and the truth of His word, we will find that there are some things and people that we will be drawing away from. Not all unity is a good thing. If you put a cat, a pit bull dog, a mouse, a cobra, and a little girl all in one eight by eight room, your "unity" is going to get very ugly! Those things simply do not agree. Our unity is to be a unity built on the truth of the Word of God. The closer someone is to the truth of the Word, the greater our unity. The farther away someone is from the truth of the Word, the greater our separation. It is not complicated; it is just the "law of mixed fabrics."

Chapter Two
The Qualifications of the Priesthood

Leviticus 21:16 *And the LORD spake unto Moses, saying,* **17** *Speak unto Aaron, saying, Whosoever he be of thy seed in their generations that hath any blemish, let him not approach to offer the bread of his God.* **18** *For whatsoever man he be that hath a blemish, he shall not approach: a blind man, or a lame, or he that hath a flat nose, or any thing superfluous,* **19** *Or a man that is brokenfooted, or brokenhanded,* **20** *Or crookbackt, or a dwarf, or that hath a blemish in his eye, or be scurvy, or scabbed, or hath his stones broken;* **21** *No man that hath a blemish of the seed of Aaron the priest shall come nigh to offer the offerings of the LORD made by fire: he hath a blemish; he shall not come nigh to offer the bread of his God.* **22** *He shall eat the bread of his God, both of the most holy, and of the holy.* **23** *Only he shall not go in unto the vail, nor come nigh unto the altar, because he hath a blemish; that he profane not my sanctuaries: for I the LORD do sanctify them.* **24** *And Moses told it unto Aaron, and to his sons, and unto all the children of Israel.*

Well, it appears that God has never consulted the Americans with Disabilities Act.

In speaking of the priesthood, He eliminated quite a few people from being able to serve within the holy place! Here is the list of people who were forbidden from serving:

- Blind
- Lame
- Flat nosed (How flat does it have to be to be flat? Let's compare…)
- Anything superfluous (More than you should have of something, like six fingers, six toes, three eyes, etc.)
- Broken footed (also signifies a deformity of the foot)
- Broken handed (also signifies a deformity of the hand)
- Crookbackt (hunchback)
- Dwarf
- Blemished in the eye
- Scurvy (here means a skin problem to cause excess itching)
- Scabbed (Like half of the youth group at my church)
- Broken stones (If any young person is reading this, do not write me for an explanation. Ask your parents; that is what they are there for, to answer uncomfortable questions. Trust me, they love it.)

Summarizing this list, commentator Adam Clarke said:

> "The priest with a blemish was not permitted to enter into the holy of holies, nor to burn incense, nor to offer the shew-bread nor to light the golden candlestick, &c. In short, he was not permitted to perform any essential function of the priesthood." (1:581)

Go ahead and admit it. Reading this, you think God sounds like a big bully, and that there is a Country Club mentality being promoted. It certainly sounds like it, does it not? What does this "odd" passage of Scripture mean? There have been many interesting opinions given concerning it. Listen to Adam Clarke's opinion once again:

> "Never was a wiser, a more rational, and a more expedient law enacted relative to sacred matters. The man who ministers in holy

things, who professes to be the interpreter of the will of God, should have nothing in his person nor in his manner which cannot contribute to render him respectable in the eyes of those to whom he ministers. If on the contrary, he has any personal defect, anything that may render him contemptible or despicable, his usefulness will be greatly injured, if not entirely prevented. If, however, a man have received any damage in the work of God, by persecution or otherwise, his scars are honourable, and will add to his respectability. But if he be received into the ministry with any of the blemishes specified here, he never will and never can have that respect which is essentially necessary to secure his usefulness. Let no man say this is a part of the Mosaic law, and we are not bound by it. It is an eternal law, founded on reason, propriety, common sense, and absolute necessity. The priest, the prophet, the Christian minister, is the representative of Jesus Christ; let nothing in his person, carriage, or doctrine, be unworthy of the personage he represents. A deformed person, though consummate in diplomatic wisdom, would never be employed as an ambassador by any enlightened court, if any fit person, unblemished, could possibly be procured." (1:581)

Did you understand that? If not, read it again, carefully. Mr. Clarke's opinion is that the regulations given here in Leviticus for the priests are fully applicable and to be fully enforced today in the ministry of the church. If he is right, think through that list and consider all of the great men of God, mightily used by His hand, that must be viewed as disqualified!

What was the point of this law? Does God discriminate on surface matters? Is He heartless and cruel? What can we learn from it?

The requirements for a Christian minister are found in I Timothy 3:1-7, and do not even mention appearance.

A priest is not a pastor; a pastor is not a priest. The priesthood was never listed in Scripture as an office of the church. Not one of these qualifications was ever repeated in the New Testament. Here are the qualifications for a minister in a New Testament church:

1 Timothy 3:1 *This is a true saying, If a man desire the office of a bishop, he desireth a good work.* **2** *A bishop then must be blameless, the husband of one wife, vigilant, sober, of good behaviour, given to hospitality, apt to teach;* **3** *Not given to wine, no striker, not greedy of filthy lucre; but patient, not a brawler, not covetous;* **4** *One that ruleth well his own house, having his children in subjection with all gravity;* **5** *(For if a man know not how to rule his own house, how shall he take care of the church of God?)* **6** *Not a novice, lest being lifted up with pride he fall into the condemnation of the devil.* **7** *Moreover he must have a good report of them which are without; lest he fall into reproach and the snare of the devil.*

In all of the qualifications for a New Testament church minister, there was not one mention of physical characteristics. Every item was about character and behavior.

Paul was described as "weak" in bodily presence - 2 Corinthians 10:10

2 Corinthians 10:10 *For his letters, say they, are weighty and powerful; but his bodily presence is weak* (meaning infirmed, feeble), *and his speech contemptible.*

If these qualifications are binding for a New Testament preacher, then Paul himself was disqualified.

Once again please remember that the entire Old Testament had a purpose:

Romans 15:4 *For whatsoever things were written aforetime were written for our learning, that we through patience and comfort of the scriptures might have hope.*

Those requirements on the priests pointed to something way beyond themselves. Many of the things God commanded in the Old Testament are looked at as if they are sledgehammers when in reality they are paint brushes. This is one of those Divine paint brushes, and the picture it painted was high, holy, and specific to exactly one person.

Jesus is our Great High Priest

Hebrews 3:1 *Wherefore, holy brethren, partakers of the heavenly calling, consider the Apostle and High Priest of our profession, Christ Jesus;*

Hebrews 4:14 *Seeing then that we have a great high priest, that is passed into the heavens, Jesus the Son of God, let us hold fast our profession.* **15** *For we have not an high priest which cannot be touched with the feeling of our infirmities; but was in all points tempted like as we are, yet without sin.*

Hebrews 6:20 *Whither the forerunner is for us entered, even Jesus, made an high priest for ever after the order of Melchisedec.*

Hebrews 8:1 *Now of the things which we have spoken this is the sum: We have such an high priest, who is set on the right hand of the throne of the Majesty in the heavens;*

Just as the children of Israel had a high priest that would enter into the Holy Place and intercede for them, we have a High Priest, Jesus Christ, that enters into the Holy Place before the Father and intercedes for us. Just as the Old Testament priests were required to be without blemish, our great High Priest had to be without blemish as well.

In verses seventeen through twenty-three of our text, the word blemish occurs six times. God was very serious about this. Blemishes that could be seen disqualified the priest: blind, lame, flat nosed, superfluous, broken footed, broken handed, crooked back, dwarf, a blemish in his eye. Blemishes that could not be seen, or that could be hidden, still disqualified the priest: scurvy, scabbed, stones broken.

The intercessor could not have a blemish, seen or unseen. He must be without flaw.

Hebrews 7:26 *For such an high priest became us, who is holy, harmless, **undefiled**, separate from sinners, and made higher than the heavens;*

Jesus, our Great High Priest, is without any of the flaws specified in Leviticus.

Consider:

Blindness would indicate that He could not see, yet our Great High Priest sees everything:

Proverbs 15:3 *The eyes of the LORD are in every place, beholding the evil and the good.*

Lame would indicate that He had difficulty getting around, yet our Great High Priest is everywhere at all times:

Psalm 139:7 *Whither shall I go from thy spirit? or whither shall I flee from thy presence? **8** If I ascend up into heaven, thou art there: if I make my bed in hell, behold, thou art there.*

Flat nosed would indicate that He has difficulty smelling, yet our Great High Priest has no difficulty smelling the sweet savor of a godly life:

2 Corinthians 2:15 *For we are unto God a sweet savour of Christ, in them that are saved, and in them that perish:*

Superfluous would indicate that there are things about God that are unnecessary. Yet our great High Priest is perfectly proportioned, having the perfect balance of mercy, grace, love, justice, and making it all fit together properly. And no wonder, considering what Paul told the church at Colosse concerning Him:

Colossians 2:9 *For in him dwelleth all the fulness of the Godhead bodily.*

Broken footed would indicate that He cannot walk well. Yet our Great High priest walks in ways and places that no one else can. In Daniel 3, He walked in the midst of the fire. In Revelation 2, He walks in the midst of the seven candlesticks (churches). In Psalm 23, He walks with us through the valley of the shadow of death.

Broken handed would indicate that He has lost some of His power. Yet our Great High Priest has the most powerful of all hands.

Powerful enough to save:

Isaiah 59:1 *Behold, the LORD'S hand is not shortened, that it cannot save; neither his ear heavy, that it cannot hear:*

Powerful enough to judge:

Daniel 4:35 *And all the inhabitants of the earth are reputed as nothing: and he doeth according to his will in the army of heaven, and among the inhabitants of the earth: and none can stay his hand, or say unto him, What doest thou?*

Crookbackt would indicate a weakness or deformity of His back, yet our Great High Priest has a back strong enough and perfect enough to take our stripes upon Himself:

Isaiah 53:5 *But he was wounded for our transgressions, he was bruised for our iniquities: the chastisement of our peace was upon him; and with his stripes we are healed.*

Isaiah 50:6 *I gave my back to the smiters, and my cheeks to them that plucked off the hair: I hid not my face from shame and spitting.*

Dwarf would indicate a lack of stature, yet our Great High Priest is above all:

Hebrews 7:26 *For such an high priest became us, who is holy, harmless, undefiled, separate from sinners, and made higher than the heavens;*

Blemished in the eye would indicate that He could see, but He might not see properly; His vision might deceive

Him. Yet our Great High Priest sees with a clarity that no man could ever have:

1 Samuel 16:7 *But the LORD said unto Samuel, Look not on his countenance, or on the height of his stature; because I have refused him: for the LORD seeth not as man seeth; for man looketh on the outward appearance, but the LORD looketh on the heart.*

Scurvy would indicate a problem with the skin, a problem with the flesh. Our Great High Priest had no problem at all with the flesh:

Hebrews 4:15 *For we have not an high priest which cannot be touched with the feeling of our infirmities; but was in all points tempted like as we are, yet without sin.*

Scabbed would indicate a festering wound. Our Great High Priest does not have scabs, He has prints, scars:

John 20:25 *The other disciples therefore said unto him, We have seen the Lord. But he said unto them, Except I shall see in his hands the print of the nails, and put my finger into the **print** of the nails, and thrust my hand into his side, I will not believe. 26 And after eight days again his disciples were within, and Thomas with them: then came Jesus, the doors being shut, and stood in the midst, and said, Peace be unto you. 27 Then saith he to Thomas, Reach hither thy finger, and behold my hands...*

Broken stones would indicate that He cannot reproduce. Our Great High Priest has no problem reproducing:

1 John 3:1a *Behold, what manner of love the Father hath bestowed upon us, that we should be called the sons of God...*

You see, if we apply Leviticus 21 to ourselves, we are missing the point entirely. We cannot perfectly fulfill these requirements, but our Great High Priest can.

Chapter Three
He Died for Picking Up Sticks

Numbers 15:32 *And while the children of Israel were in the wilderness, they found a man that gathered sticks upon the sabbath day.* **33** *And they that found him gathering sticks brought him unto Moses and Aaron, and unto all the congregation.* **34** *And they put him in ward, because it was not declared what should be done to him.* **35** *And the LORD said unto Moses, The man shall be surely put to death: all the congregation shall stone him with stones without the camp.* **36** *And all the congregation brought him without the camp, and stoned him with stones, and he died; as the LORD commanded Moses.*

The seeming overreaction

The facts here are not mysterious. There are times when things are not as they seem, times when a word study perhaps changes what we thought we knew. This is not one of those times. This man engaged in one very simple act; he gathered sticks on the Sabbath day.

That one simple act got him killed.

There are many things that the Old Testament prescribes the death penalty for that are clearly of a vile and egregious nature:

Murder:

Numbers 35:16 *And if he smite him with an instrument of iron, so that he die, he is a murderer: the murderer shall surely be put to death.* **17** *And if he smite him with throwing a stone, wherewith he may die, and he die, he is a murderer: the murderer shall surely be put to death.* **18** *Or if he smite him with an hand weapon of wood, wherewith he may die, and he die, he is a murderer: the murderer shall surely be put to death.*

Kidnapping:

Exodus 21:16 *And he that stealeth a man, and selleth him, or if he be found in his hand, he shall surely be put to death.*

Bestiality:

Exodus 22:19 *Whosoever lieth with a beast shall surely be put to death.*

Sacrificing babies to Molech:

Leviticus 20:2 *Again, thou shalt say to the children of Israel, Whosoever he be of the children of Israel, or of the strangers that sojourn in Israel, that giveth any of his seed unto Molech; he shall surely be put to death: the people of the land shall stone him with stones.*

This is not all of the list, but it is a good representation. So again, there were many reasons that people could be put to death that were overwhelmingly awful. But in this case, it was not anything like any of those things. This was a man picking up sticks on the Sabbath Day, and it cost him his life. And this was our God who commanded it.

Do you see why the critic or the person who has not done his homework would be quick to beat the Bible and Bible believers with this passage? At first blush, it certainly **seems** to the human eye to be very harsh, a severe overreaction.

The scriptural clarity on the issue

I am not yet going to tell you why it made sense for the man to die, but I am going to show you right now just how very clear the commandment was that he broke.

Exodus 31:14 *Ye shall keep the sabbath therefore; for it is holy unto you: every one that defileth it shall surely be put to death: for whosoever doeth any work therein, that soul shall be cut off from among his people.* **15** *Six days may work be done; but in the seventh is the sabbath of rest, holy to the LORD: whosoever doeth any work in the sabbath day, he shall surely be put to death.*

Exodus 35:2 *Six days shall work be done, but on the seventh day there shall be to you an holy day, a sabbath of rest to the LORD: whosoever doeth work therein shall be put to death.* **3** *Ye shall kindle no fire throughout your habitations upon the sabbath day.*

There are many things we do not know about this man who died. We do not know how old he was, or what tribe he was from, or if he was married, or if he had money, or if he was attractive.

One thing we do know about him, though, is that he was not simply "caught off guard" by all of this. Everybody in the entire nation knew what was written on those stone tablets that God gave to Moses. And one of the things that was clearly spelled out, then spoken to the people, then reiterated over and over again, was that the people were not allowed to do work on the Sabbath Day. And one of the very specific things they were not to do was to kindle a fire, and that is the only reason at all for this man to have been gathering sticks. They were not building houses out there in the wilderness.

When this man violated the law of God on this issue, it was not some obscure thing that no one knew about. In fact, he had two million or so reasons not to do what he was doing. Can you figure out what I mean by that?

Everyone else was either in their tents or resting and worshiping somewhere outside of their tents, no one else was doing any work at all. No one else was gathering sticks. The fact that everyone else in the nation knew and understood and was demonstrating what not to do means that this man had no excuse at all. Both from the written and reiterated law and from the behavior of everyone else, it was very clear that he was not supposed to be doing what he was doing.

The setting of the offense

We have already begun to hint at this just a moment ago, but let us begin to really fill it out. What this man did was not done in a vacuum or on an island. There was a definite time and place for what he did, and it makes a difference.

Let us, first of all, see if we can establish a time factor. Look at what is recorded just before this episode of chapter fifteen.

Numbers 13:1 *And the LORD spake unto Moses, saying,* **2** *Send thou men, that they may search the land of Canaan, which I give unto the children of Israel: of every tribe of their fathers shall ye send a man, every one a ruler among them.*

Numbers 13 is only several months removed from the Exodus. Two years at most. It is in Numbers 13 that Moses sent out the spies to examine the land. They came back, and here is what happened:

Numbers 13:25 *And they returned from searching of the land after forty days.* **26** *And they went and came to Moses, and to Aaron, and to all the congregation of the children of Israel, unto the wilderness of Paran, to Kadesh; and brought back word unto them, and unto all the congregation, and shewed them the fruit of the land.* **27** *And they told him, and said, We came unto the land whither thou sentest us, and surely it floweth with milk and honey; and this is the fruit of it.* **28** *Nevertheless the people be strong that* *dwell in the land, and the cities are walled, and very great: and moreover we saw the children of Anak there.* **29** *The Amalekites dwell in the land of the south: and the Hittites, and the Jebusites, and the Amorites, dwell in the mountains: and the Canaanites dwell by the sea, and by the coast of Jordan.* **30** *And Caleb stilled the people before Moses, and said, Let us go up at once, and possess it; for we are well able to overcome it.* **31** *But the men that went up with him said, We be not able to go up against the people; for they are stronger than we.* **32** *And they brought up an evil report of the land which they had searched unto the children of Israel, saying, The land, through which we have gone to search it, is a land that eateth up the inhabitants thereof; and all the people that we saw in it are men of a great stature.* **33** *And there we saw the giants, the sons of Anak, which come of the giants: and we were in our own sight as grasshoppers, and so we were in their sight.*

Numbers 14:1 *And all the congregation lifted up their voice, and cried; and the people wept that night.* **2** *And all the children of Israel murmured against Moses and against Aaron: and the whole congregation said unto them, Would God that we had died in the land of Egypt! or would God we had died in this wilderness!* **3** *And wherefore hath the LORD brought us unto this land, to fall by the sword, that our wives and our children should be a prey? were it not better for us to return into Egypt?* **4** *And they said one to another, Let us make a captain, and let us return into Egypt.* **5** *Then Moses and Aaron fell on their faces before all the assembly of the congregation of the children of Israel.* **6** *And Joshua the son of Nun, and Caleb the son of Jephunneh, which were of them that searched the land, rent their clothes:* **7** *And they spake unto all the company of the children of Israel, saying, The land, which we passed through to search it, is an exceeding good land.* **8** *If the LORD delight in us, then he will bring us into this land, and give it us; a land which floweth with milk and honey.* **9** *Only rebel not ye against the LORD,* *neither fear ye the people of the land; for they are bread for us: their defence is departed from them, and the LORD is with us: fear them not.* **10** *But all the congregation bade stone them with stones. And the glory of the LORD appeared in the tabernacle of the congregation before all the children of Israel.* **11** *And the LORD said unto Moses, How long will this people provoke me? and how long will it be ere they believe me, for all the signs which I have shewed among them?* **12** *I will smite them with the pestilence, and disinherit them, and will make of thee a greater nation and mightier than they.* **13** *And Moses said unto the LORD, Then the Egyptians shall hear it, (for thou broughtest up this people in thy might from among them;)* **14** *And they will tell it to the inhabitants of this land: for they have heard that thou LORD art among this people, that thou LORD art seen face to face, and that thy cloud standeth over them, and that thou goest before them, by day time in a pillar of a cloud, and in a pillar of fire by night.* **15** *Now if thou shalt kill all this people as one man, then the nations which have heard the fame of thee will speak, saying,* **16** *Because the LORD was not able to bring this people into the land which he sware unto them, therefore he hath slain them in the wilderness.* **17** *And now, I beseech thee, let the power of my Lord be great, according as thou hast spoken, saying,* **18** *The LORD is longsuffering, and of great mercy, forgiving iniquity and transgression, and by no means clearing the guilty, visiting the iniquity of the fathers upon the children unto the third and fourth generation.* **19** *Pardon, I beseech thee, the iniquity of this people according unto the greatness of thy mercy, and as thou hast forgiven this people, from Egypt even until now.* **20** *And the LORD said, I have pardoned according to thy word:* **21** *But as truly as I live, all the earth shall be filled with the glory of the LORD.* **22** *Because all those men which have seen my glory, and my miracles, which I did in Egypt and in the wilderness, and have tempted me now these ten times, and have not hearkened to my voice;* **23** *Surely they shall not see the land which I* *sware unto their fathers, neither shall any of them that provoked me see it:* **24** *But my servant Caleb, because he had another spirit with him, and hath followed me fully, him will I bring into the land whereinto he went; and his seed shall possess it.* **25** *(Now the Amalekites and the Canaanites dwelt in the valley.) To morrow turn you, and get you into the wilderness by the way of the Red sea.* **26** *And the LORD spake unto Moses and unto Aaron, saying,* **27** *How long shall I bear with this evil congregation, which murmur against me? I have heard the murmurings of the children of Israel, which they murmur against me.* **28** *Say unto them, As truly as I live, saith the LORD, as ye have spoken in mine ears, so will I do to you:* **29** *Your carcases shall fall in this wilderness; and all that were numbered of you, according to your whole number, from twenty years old and upward, which have murmured against me,* **30** *Doubtless ye shall not come into the land, concerning which I sware to make you dwell therein, save Caleb the son of Jephunneh, and Joshua the son of Nun.* **31** *But your little ones, which ye said should be a prey, them will I bring in, and they shall know the land which ye have despised.* **32** *But as for you, your carcases, they shall fall in this wilderness.* **33** *And your children shall wander in the wilderness forty years, and bear your whoredoms, until your carcases be wasted in the wilderness.* **34** *After the number of the days in which ye searched the land, even forty days, each day for a year, shall ye bear your iniquities, even forty years, and ye shall know my breach of promise.* **35** *I the LORD have said, I will surely do it unto all this evil congregation, that are gathered together against me: in this wilderness they shall be consumed, and there they shall die.* **36** *And the men, which Moses sent to search the land, who returned, and made all the congregation to murmur against him, by bringing up a slander upon the land,* **37** *Even those men that did bring up the evil report upon the land, died by the plague before the LORD.*

That is chapter thirteen and fourteen. As we get into chapter fifteen, some commentators outsmart themselves and say that chapter fifteen actually took place near the end of the wilderness wanderings. They are as wrong as they can be. Look what happens and what is said in chapter sixteen:

Numbers 16:1 *Now Korah, the son of Izhar, the son of Kohath, the son of Levi, and Dathan and Abiram, the sons of Eliab, and On, the son of Peleth, sons of Reuben, took men:* **2** *And they rose up before Moses, with certain of the children of Israel, two hundred and fifty princes of the assembly, famous in the congregation, men of renown:* **3** *And they gathered themselves together against Moses and against Aaron, and said unto them, Ye take too much upon you, seeing all the congregation are holy, every one of them, and the LORD is among them: wherefore then lift ye up yourselves above the congregation of the LORD?* **4** *And when Moses heard it, he fell upon his face:* **5** *And he spake unto Korah and unto all his company, saying, Even to morrow the LORD will shew who are his, and who is holy; and will cause him to come near unto him: even him whom he hath chosen will he cause to come near unto him.* **6** *This do; Take you censers, Korah, and all his company;* **7** *And put fire therein, and put incense in them before the LORD to morrow: and it shall be that the man whom the LORD doth choose, he shall be holy: ye take too much upon you, ye sons of Levi.* **8** *And Moses said unto Korah, Hear, I pray you, ye sons of Levi:* **9** *Seemeth it but a small thing unto you, that the God of Israel hath separated you from the congregation of Israel, to bring you near to himself to do the service of the tabernacle of the LORD, and to stand before the congregation to minister unto them?* **10** *And he hath brought thee near to him, and all thy brethren the sons of Levi with thee: and seek ye the priesthood also?* **11** *For which cause both thou and all thy company are gathered together against the LORD: and what is Aaron, that ye murmur against him?* **12** *And Moses sent to call Dathan and Abiram, the sons of Eliab: which said, We* *will not come up:* **13** *Is it a small thing that thou hast brought us up out of a land that floweth with milk and honey, to kill us in the wilderness, except thou make thyself altogether a prince over us?* **14** *Moreover thou hast not brought us into a land that floweth with milk and honey, or given us inheritance of fields and vineyards: wilt thou put out the eyes of these men? we will not come up.*

We know how this part of the story ended, the earth swallowing these rebels alive into hell. But the important thing for us to consider in this study is what Dathan and Abiram said: *Is it a small thing that thou hast brought us up out of a land that floweth with milk and honey, to kill us in the wilderness, except thou make thyself altogether a prince over us? Moreover thou hast not brought us into a land that floweth with milk and honey, or given us inheritance of fields and vineyards.*

Their complaint was that Moses had taken them out of Canaan, which is what just happened in chapter fourteen. Forget for a second that they themselves were at fault, not Moses. Pay attention to the fact that chapter thirteen and fourteen and fifteen and sixteen all happened right there together. This man who died for picking up sticks died at a very specific time. And what time was that?

Just a few months after he saw with his own eyes God level Egypt with plagues.

Just a few months after he saw with his own eyes God part the Red Sea.

Just a few months after he saw the thunder and lightning on Mount Sinai.

Just a few **days** after he saw a great number of people miraculously consumed with a plague for their rebellion and their following of the ten cowardly spies.

This man was in the middle of a time period when God was making Himself and His authority and His power more clearly and visibly known than at any previous time in human history! And it was then that he chose to disobey. But there is one more aspect of time to notice. Right before this man did what he did, look what God said. Our text, this account of the man dying, started with verse thirty-two. But look at the two verses right before that:

Numbers 15:30 *But the soul that doeth ought presumptuously, whether he be born in the land, or a stranger, the same reproacheth the LORD; and that soul shall be cut off from among his people. 31 Because he hath despised the word of the LORD, and hath broken his commandment, that soul shall utterly be cut off; his iniquity shall be upon him.*

In the verses leading up to verses thirty and thirty-one, God had been talking about sins of ignorance. Then in verses thirty and thirty-one, He changed gears and dealt with sins of presumption, sins where people knew they were doing wrong and were just doing it to stick their finger in the eye of authority. And immediately after that the man went out and started picking up sticks.

This man had one thing in mind: rebellion. "God said it, and I am going to do it anyway just to shove it in His face."

But there is also the place to consider. And what place would that be? That, too, I hinted at earlier. When this man chose to disobey, it was right there with two million others who were, for the briefest of moments, obeying! This was one of those ultra-rare times when they were actually not rebelling, and this man chose that moment to stir the pot.

Was it a small thing? Yes and no. How many of you have had kids behave like little demons all day long until your patience is about to snap in a million tiny pieces? Then for a time they finally settle down, and all is well... briefly. How many of you have then had one of those kids intentionally do some tiny little thing, the straw that breaks the camel's back, something to stir everyone back up, and then had them react in shock, wondering why you were so upset? Now you are beginning to understand the setting.

The stubbornness demonstrated

It should be clear by now that what this man did was not some innocent oversight.

The law was incredibly clear, the only thing they did not know was *how* he was supposed to die, which is why verse thirty-four says "*it was not declared what should be done to him.*" He violated a clear law, and he did so intentionally.

He did it during the day time, where everyone could see him.

He did it just months after the Exodus, and the Red Sea, and Mount Sinai.

He did it right after the rebellion of the spies and the death of many by the plague.

This was not some innocent man who accidentally did some trivial thing and lost his life for it. This was absolutely intentional; it was stubbornness and rebellion.

The stunning missed detail

I am forty-four years old at the time I am writing this book, and in all my years of hearing preaching and teaching there is one aspect of this I have never heard mentioned. There was something in the camp that, honestly, is so important as to make everything else we have said seem almost unimportant by comparison. Look at this:

Exodus 13:21 *And the LORD went before them by day in a pillar of a cloud, to lead them the way; and by night in a pillar of fire, to give them light; to go by day and night:* **22** *He took not away the pillar of the cloud by day, nor the pillar of fire by night, from before the people.*

The visible, miraculous, Shekinah glory of God, showing up during the daytime as a pillar, a column of a cloud coming down from heaven and resting over the tabernacle, and during the night time as a pillar, a column of fire, was right there at all times. When this man picked up his sticks, he did so right in the shadow of that presence. It was still there in Numbers 14:14, right before this happened. This man did what he did in the presence of God; he did it right to God's face. Every time he leaned over for a stick, it was an intentional challenge; it was a man daring God in the sight of everybody else to do something about it.

And now you know why a man died, "just for picking up sticks."

Chapter Four
The Plutonium of the Old Testament: Slavery

This subject, slavery in the Old Testament, is, for the critic, the biggest stick they have to swing. Let me make you a promise. If you debate a skeptic on almost any subject, and you use any Old Testament passages to prove your point, I promise you that it will not take them long at all to turn the subject to slavery.

When the debate over "gay marriage" hit the newspaper in my hometown, it took a lady, we will call her Penelope, exactly one paragraph to start talking about slavery in the Old Testament. It will be the exact same no matter what sin you point out as sin using any Old Testament passage. And if you listen to the skeptic without knowing your Bible, you will quickly come to the faulty conclusion that the Old Testament law is probably eighty to ninety percent about slavery. To hear the critics tell it, you are going to be hard-pressed to find any of the Old Testament law that is not endorsing slavery.

That said, let us look at our text verses for this chapter and find out the truth.

Jeremiah 2:14 *Is Israel a servant? is he a homeborn **slave**? why is he spoiled?*

Revelation 18:13 *And cinnamon, and odours, and ointments, and frankincense, and wine, and oil, and fine flour,* *and wheat, and beasts, and sheep, and horses, and chariots, and **slaves**, and souls of men.*

Do you know what is significant about those two verses? They are the only two times in the King James Bible that any form of the word slave is found. There is also something very significant in where they are found, namely that neither one was in the law. In fact, only one of the two, fifty percent, was even found in the Old Testament. The second of our text verses was found in the book of the Revelation.

There are other words used in the Bible that people can point to and try to demonstrate slavery, and we will look at many of those words and many of those references. But there is, I believe, a very good reason why our English Bible does not use the word slavery in regard to what we see in the law: because what we know as slavery bears little to no resemblance at all to what people point to in the Bible as slavery.

When we think of slavery, and when the critics claim that God endorsed slavery, let me tell you what people are thinking of: they are thinking of slavery in America prior to the Emancipation Proclamation.

They are thinking of boatloads of people who were living peacefully thousands of miles away from here, not fighting against our country at all, who were stolen from Africa and brought here against their will. They are thinking of whips and chains and humans being reduced to cattle. They are thinking of people who worked but were not paid. They are thinking of people who tried to escape but were dragged back. They are thinking of abuse and cruelty. And please pay close attention: there is no justification for any of that to ever happen. Slavery was wicked, period. But that type of slavery did not exist in Israel, and was, in fact, forbidden by God in the Old Testament law.

Let us look at what we see in the Old Testament on this subject. Before we do, let me tell you what you will find and what you will not find. You will find some things that make your modern Western mind a bit uncomfortable, at least until they are explained. But what you will not find is an equivalent to what we know as slavery; people stolen from their land, taken to another land, treated like cattle, used and abused, working for no pay, and trying to escape yet being dragged back.

A choice of terms

Let us begin by examining the terms used on this subject. The critics will almost universally use the term slavery in regard to what they see in the Old Testament law. But that is not the terms we find in Scripture. Here, though, are the terms we do find.

Servant:

Exodus 12:44 *But every man's **servant** that is bought for money, when thou hast circumcised him, then shall he eat thereof.*

Maid:

Exodus 21:20 *And if a man smite his servant, or his **maid**, with a rod, and he die under his hand; he shall be surely punished.*

Manservant and maidservant:

Exodus 21:32 *If the ox shall push a **manservant** or a **maidservant**; he shall give unto their master thirty shekels of silver, and the ox shall be stoned.*

Bondmen and bondmaids:

Leviticus 25:44 *Both thy **bondmen**, and thy **bondmaids**, which thou shalt have, shall be of the heathen that are round about you; of them shall ye buy bondmen and bondmaids.*

These are the actual terms used in the law. I am curious: why would the critics make a conscious choice to use the word slavery rather than any of the actual words used? The answer is not hard to figure out. They do so because it suits their desire better, it fits their goals better. Their desire and goal is to make God and the Bible look bad, and they can accomplish that much more easily by using a word like "slave" rather than a word like "servant."

A context to broaden

Something that the critic very regularly fails to do is to look outside of the box he has built. And to make matters worse, they always build too small of a box. In this instance, what I mean is that the critic is going to find one or two verses that sound mean to them, build a box around it, shine a light on it, and then demand that the entire world look at it through a microscope.

But why don't we start from much farther out and work our way in? After all, doesn't it stand to reason that the more information we have to work with, the more accurate of a conclusion we can arrive at?

That being the case, let us expand our view out to both sides of the law, pre and post.

Pre-law, what do we find? We find that God made man perfect and that if man had never sinned, nothing unpleasant would ever have entered earth or humanity, including slavery. God made all of humanity free, and slavery was a man-made invention. Furthermore, neither Jews nor Christians were even close to being the first ones to practice any form of it. You might also want to remember that God Himself has never enslaved anyone, each and every person who signs on to serve Him does so of his or her own free will!

Post-law, what do we find? We find that the New Testament church in Jerusalem was a body of believers who were one hundred percent equal regardless of their skin color. Look at what Peter said:

Acts 10:34 *Then Peter opened his mouth, and said, Of a truth I perceive that God is no respecter of persons: 35 But in every nation he that feareth him, and worketh righteousness, is accepted with him.*

The New Testament church was made up of people from all nations and all skin colors. One of the first seven deacons, Nicholas, was a Greek proselyte, not a Jew (Acts 6:5)

Acts 13:1 says *Now there were in the church that was at Antioch certain prophets and teachers; as Barnabas, and Simeon that was called Niger...*

That word Niger means black. There was a black man in the early church who not only was not a slave, he was actually regarded as a prophet and teacher.

Peter went on to say this:

Acts 17:26 *And hath made of one blood all nations of men for to dwell on all the face of the earth, and hath determined the times before appointed, and the bounds of their habitation;*

Peter, in the New Testament, spoke of the fact that the God of the Old Testament made everyone from the same man and the same blood.

We further find a rather unique scene in heaven:

Revelation 7:9 *After this I beheld, and, lo, a great multitude, which no man could number, of all **nations**, and **kindreds**, and **people**, and **tongues**, stood before the throne, and before the Lamb, clothed with white robes, and palms in their hands;*

So, before the law, we have a God showing no sign of approving what we know as slavery, and after the law, we have a God showing no sign of approving what we know as slavery. Even the instructions later given by Paul for servants to obey their masters was an indication not of God's approval of slavery as an institution but of a what the proper heart attitude was to be in a pre-established situation.

A condition of man

We have already pretty well established that what we know of as slavery is something God never caused or endorsed. But we still need to deal with what people refer to as slavery in the Old Testament, even though it should be called servitude, not slavery.

There were conditions in mankind that necessitated the servitude of the Old Testament. When those conditions are understood, much of that servitude actually will be seen as a kind thing rather than as a cruel thing. The most common reason for servitude in the Old Testament was when a person fell on very hard times and needed some help:

Leviticus 25:39 *And if thy brother that dwelleth by thee be waxen poor, and be sold unto thee; thou shalt not compel him to serve as a bondservant:* **40** *But as an hired servant, and as a sojourner, he shall be with thee, and shall serve thee unto the year of jubilee:*

This issue of poverty was a constant problem. But here is what the critic will not likely tell you: God even made provision for that, thus making servitude a very rare thing indeed. Look at some of the provision He made:

A piece of equipment necessary for the family to work and survive could not be taken as collateral for a loan.

Deuteronomy 24:6 *No man shall take the nether or the upper millstone to pledge: for he taketh a man's life to pledge.*

A person could likely get a very good deal on a good millstone if someone got desperate enough. But God forbid them from doing so. Here is another part of that provision:

A poor man's cloak that had been used as collateral had to be returned by nightfall, and a widow's cloak could not be taken at all.

Deuteronomy 24:12 *And if the man be poor, thou shalt not sleep with his pledge:* **13** *In any case thou shalt deliver him the pledge again when the sun goeth down, that he may sleep in his own raiment, and bless thee: and it shall be righteousness unto thee before the LORD thy God.*

Deuteronomy 24:17 *Thou shalt not pervert the judgment of the stranger, nor of the fatherless; nor take a widow's raiment to pledge:*

Here is yet a third part of that provision:

The crops were never to be fully harvested, there was always to be some left behind for the poor.

Deuteronomy 24:19 *When thou cuttest down thine harvest in thy field, and hast forgot a sheaf in the field, thou shalt not go again to fetch it: it shall be for the stranger, for the fatherless, and for the widow: that the LORD thy God may bless thee in all the work of thine hands. 20 When thou beatest thine olive tree, thou shalt not go over the boughs again: it shall be for the stranger, for the fatherless, and for the widow. 21 When thou gatherest the grapes of thy vineyard, thou shalt not glean it afterward: it shall be for the stranger, for the fatherless, and for the widow.*

God ensured that the poor would always have wheat and olives and grapes. God ensured that the poor would always have their warm clothes to sleep in and that they would always have their equipment to work with. And yet this is the God who gets accused of being a slave trader.

Did people go into servitude? Yes. Was it something that should have been necessary? Not very often. God made a way for people who wanted to to be able to do three things: work, sleep, and eat. May I point out what should be obvious? After spending trillions of dollars in the "war on poverty," we in our modern, enlightened age are still miles behind ancient Israel in this matter.

But the condition of man and the condition of the sinful world that man has developed made it such that sometimes, even those generous provisions were not enough. And that is where servitude came in.

A clear look at the "slavery" of the Old Testament

The reason the critics love to harp on slavery is that, quite honestly, they know that it will embarrass Christians. How can we defend a God who ostensibly is no better than some plantation owner in the deep south, using and abusing human beings?

But the reason they do not love it when people actually pick up their Bibles and study it for themselves is that they know that when the actual details are given, they will be the ones that are embarrassed because it wasn't anything at all like the picture they are painting.

So, let us paint our own picture, an accurate picture. And let us begin with the number one, most important fact you will ever have on this subject, the one thing you must never forget:

No human being was ever allowed to be kidnaped and enslaved.

Exodus 21:16 *And he that stealeth a man, and selleth him, or if he be found in his hand, he shall surely be put to death.*

This one fact, all by itself, makes Old Testament servitude one hundred percent different from modern day slavery. The Jews were not sending ships across the waters to snatch boys out of their beds and bring them back to Israel to be enslaved. Other nations did so, but God forbid His people from doing so.

Every servant in Israel was to be paid for his work.

Deuteronomy 24:14 *Thou shalt not oppress an hired servant that is poor and needy, whether he be of thy brethren, or of thy strangers that are in thy land within thy gates:* **15** *At his day thou shalt give him his hire, neither shall the sun go down upon it; for he is poor, and setteth his heart upon it: lest he cry against thee unto the LORD, and it be sin unto thee.*

This is also one hundred percent different from modern-day slavery where slaves were regarded as pieces of equipment to be used for free and then thrown away when they were of no more use. Other nations were like that, but not the Jews. Their servants got paid.

Every servant in Israel had the ability to fully participate in family life and in holidays and feast days.

Exodus 12:43 *And the LORD said unto Moses and Aaron, This is the ordinance of the **passover**: There shall no* *stranger eat thereof:* **44** *But every man's servant that is bought for money, when thou hast circumcised him, then shall he eat thereof.*

Deuteronomy 16:13 *Thou shalt observe **the feast of tabernacles** seven days, after that thou hast gathered in thy corn and thy wine:* **14** *And thou shalt rejoice in thy feast, thou, and thy son, and thy daughter, and thy **manservant**, and thy **maidservant**, and the Levite, the stranger, and the fatherless, and the widow, that are within thy gates.*

Every so-called "slave" in Israel got the exact same amount of time off like everyone else, including their master!

Exodus 20:8 *Remember the sabbath day, to keep it holy.* **9** *Six days shalt thou labour, and do all thy work:* **10** *But the seventh day is the sabbath of the LORD thy God: in it thou shalt not do any work, thou, nor thy son, nor thy daughter, thy manservant, nor thy maidservant, nor thy cattle, nor thy stranger that is within thy gates:* **11** *For in six days the LORD made heaven and earth, the sea, and all that in them is, and rested the seventh day: wherefore the LORD blessed the sabbath day, and hallowed it.*

From the king in the palace to the "slave" in the field, everybody got one day a week completely off work.

When God spoke of injury rights, He did not grammatically limit them to freemen.

In other words, since there is no indication that those in servitude were excluded, we should conclude that both free men and "slaves" had the exact same rights if injured. Whoever injured them had to provide for their care:

Exodus 21:18 *And if men strive together, and one smite another with a stone, or with his fist, and he die not, but keepeth his bed:* **19** *If he rise again, and walk abroad upon his staff, then shall he that smote him be quit: only he shall pay for the loss of his time, and shall cause him to be thoroughly healed.*

Both free men and slaves were regarded as equal if injured by an animal in that the animal who did so was stoned.

Exodus 21:28 *If an ox gore a man or a woman, that they die: then* **the ox shall be surely stoned**, *and his flesh shall not be eaten; but the owner of the ox shall be quit.*

Exodus 21:32 *If the ox shall push a manservant or a maidservant; he shall give unto their master thirty shekels of silver, and* **the ox shall be stoned**.

In one case, "slaves" were actually treated better than most everyone else. A servant of a priest could eat the food given as offerings, but no-one else other than the priests in the entire nation could do that!

Leviticus 22:10 *There shall no stranger eat of the holy thing: a sojourner of the priest, or an hired servant, shall not eat of the holy thing.* **11** *But if the priest buy any soul with his money, he shall eat of it, and he that is born in his house: they shall eat of his meat.*

Here is another massive difference between modern slavery and what the critics decry as slavery in the Old Testament: at least for Jews, Old Testament slavery was temporary, it came with a built-in expiration date.

Exodus 21:2 *If thou buy an Hebrew servant, six years he shall serve: and in the seventh he shall go out free for nothing.*

Not only were they allowed to go free, but they were also to be generously provided for as they did:

Deuteronomy 15:12 *And if thy brother, an Hebrew man, or an Hebrew woman, be sold unto thee, and serve thee six years; then in the seventh year thou shalt let him go free from thee.* **13** *And when thou sendest him out free from thee, thou shalt not let him go away empty:* **14** *Thou shalt furnish him liberally out of thy flock, and out of thy floor, and out of thy winepress: of that wherewith the LORD thy God hath blessed thee thou shalt give unto him.* **15** *And thou shalt remember that thou wast a bondman in the land of Egypt, and* *the LORD thy God redeemed thee: therefore I command thee this thing to day.*

Another stark difference between what you see in the Old Testament and what we now call slavery is that "slaves" could also end up going free for things that no plantation owner would ever dream of setting someone free for:

Exodus 21:26 *And if a man smite the eye of his servant, or the eye of his maid, that it perish; he shall let him go free for his eye's sake.* **27** *And if he smite out his manservant's tooth, or his maidservant's tooth; he shall let him go free for his tooth's sake.*

Think of that. One tooth! Can you imagine some slave owner of the old south setting a slave free because he knocked one of his teeth out? That would never happen. They could beat their slaves literally to death, and it is unlikely that anyone one would say a word. But in Israel, if you so much as knocked a single tooth out, the law demanded that he be set free. Do you know what that resulted in? It resulted in people who very little desire to hurt their so-called "slaves."

The controversial passages examined

All of the passages I have just shown you will very consistently be ignored by the critics. But I am not going to do what they do, I am not going to point out passages that I want you to see and then hope you do not see others. I want to take some time and show you the passages that the critics are going to show you, and then I am going to explain them, which is something the critic definitely will not do.

Exodus 21:20 *And if a man smite his servant, or his maid, with a rod, and he die under his hand; he shall be surely punished.* **21** *Notwithstanding, if he continue a day or two, he shall not be punished: for he is his money.*

The first of those two verses we like, because it clearly goes right along with what we have been saying and the picture we have been painting. Servants, so-called slaves, were so precious to God that they were protected like

49

everyone else, and anyone killing them was punished. But that second verse seems like a puzzle. It seems to be saying that if a man beats a slave with a rod, and he lives a day or two before he dies, there will be no punishment because he is just a purchased piece of property to be used and then thrown away.

The key to understanding this verse is the very last phrase, "for he is his money." What that phrase did was go to a particular question that is asked whenever anyone kills anyone else, and they are trying to figure out if it was an accident or intentional. What do investigators look for to determine that? Motive.

When a master beat a servant, and he died right then, there was clearly motive, and the master himself had just forfeited his own life. But if a master beat a servant, and then the servant surprisingly died a couple of days later, the master was not charged with murder. For starters, they had no way of knowing if what the master did actually caused the servant's death. If it was clear that what he did caused the death, then the master still died, no matter how much later, because that fell under the laws about murder:

Numbers 35:18 *Or if he smite him with an hand weapon of wood, wherewith he may die, and he die, he is a murderer: the murderer shall surely be put to death.*

So again, please understand that if the master beat the servant, and the servant died a day or two later, and it was clear that the beating caused it, the master himself was put to death. Exodus 21:20-21 is not talking about that kind of a situation. It is talking about a situation where the master beat the servant, the servant seemed fine, the servant then died a day or two later, and there was no way to know if the beating caused it. In that case, the master was not punished, because, here is the motive part, "he is his money."

Do you know what that phrase means? It does not mean that the servant was just some tool that had been bought and could be abused and killed at will. What it means is that the master had no motive to kill him.

The master bought the servant by paying whatever massive debt he was under. Then the master paid him wages. Then the master provided for his needs. The master therefore had no motive to kill. If he killed the servant, he was slitting his own financial throat. You cannot get enough work out of someone to recoup your investment if that person is dead. This was the master being given the logical benefit of the doubt in a case where there was no proof that what he had done had caused the death.

Here is another of the "controversial" passages:

Exodus 21:1 *Now these are the judgments which thou shalt set before them.* **2** *If thou buy an Hebrew servant, six years he shall serve: and in the seventh he shall go out free for nothing.* **3** *If he came in by himself, he shall go out by himself: if he were married, then his wife shall go out with him.* **4** *If his master have given him a wife, and she have born him sons or daughters; the wife and her children shall be her master's, and he shall go out by himself.*

On the face of it, this seems to evoke memories of the Deep South, where a family would be forcibly separated. But let us look closer. According to verse three, if he had a wife when he came into his servitude when the time of his servitude was up, the wife got to leave as well. The family unit remained intact. There is no indication anywhere that children were not also allowed to go out free with mom and dad, they most assuredly were. So, the idea we have of a family snatched from Africa, taken down to the Deep South to work on the plantation, and then the master later busting up the family and selling off the wife and kids, was not allowed by the law of God.

Notice that word "given" in verse four. In the strictest sense of the word, were brides ever "given" in the Old Testament? Certainly not. If you wanted to marry a girl, you had to pay her father. We used to call that a dowry. Can you think of someone in Scripture who wanted to marry a girl, and had no money to do so?

That would be Jacob, who wanted to marry lovely Rachel. And what solution did he and her father settle on? Jacob had to work seven years for her. And that was actually pretty standard! You don't pay the price, you don't get the girl.

Now go back to the reason that people went into servitude, what was it? Poverty. So, could a man who was so poor that he had to go into servitude afford to pay the dowry for a wife? No. Therefore, he could not get married. Is that pleasant? No. So what would a generous master do? He would give him a wife, which could well have been one of his own daughters.

Fast forward to the end of the six-year period of servitude. The man's debt that got him into poverty has been paid, but that is all that has been paid. There has been no dowry paid to the father/master for the wife. So, the man had the option of going free and leaving her behind. But there was another option:

Exodus 21:5 *And if the servant shall plainly say, I love my master, my wife, and my children; I will not go out free: 6 Then his master shall bring him unto the judges; he shall also bring him to the door, or unto the door post; and his master shall bore his ear through with an aul; and he shall serve him for ever.*

No man ever had to be separated from his wife and kids. If he could not afford the dowry, they could all just stay there together.

Right after these verses follows another set of verses that critics love to point to without explanation:

Exodus 21:7 *And if a man sell his daughter to be a maidservant, she shall not go out as the menservants do.*

When critics point at this verse, they usually accompany it by a shrill and hysterical "SEE! YOUR GOD

ALLOWED FATHERS TO MAKE SEX SLAVES OUT OF THEIR DAUGHTERS!"

Perhaps if they would stop screaming and get their eyes to stop rolling into the back of their heads, they could actually read a few other verses that would show them how wrong they are and how silly they are being.

Why don't we start here:

Leviticus 19:29 *Do not prostitute thy daughter, to cause her to be a whore; lest the land fall to whoredom, and the land become full of wickedness.*

The very thing the critics say about Exodus 21:7 is disproved by Leviticus 19:29.

But truthfully, you would not really even have to go as far as the book of Leviticus to figure out that is not what Exodus 21:7 says. You might want to stay much closer. In fact, if you want to know what Exodus 21:7 means, you should actually start by looking at the very next verse, Exodus 21:8 and the few verses that follow.

Exodus 21:8 *If she please not her master, who hath* **betrothed** *her to himself, then shall he let her be redeemed: to sell her unto a strange nation he shall have no power, seeing he hath dealt deceitfully with her. 9 And if he have* **betrothed** *her unto his son, he shall deal with her after the manner of daughters. 10 If he take him* **another wife**; *her food, her raiment, and her duty of marriage, shall he not diminish. 11 And if he do not these three unto her, then shall she go out free without money.*

When a father from a poor family had little chance to ever make things better for his family, he could do something very unique and helpful for his family and his daughter. He could find a man that was well off and sell his daughter as a handmaid espoused to be a wife. In other words, she was too young to marry just yet, so she would be taken into that household, she would grow up there as a tenderly cared-for servant, and when she was an adult, she would be married to the master of the house.

Another variation of that is given in verse nine where she is taken into the house as a tenderly cared for-servant with the purpose of later marrying the son. That arrangement would provide for the needs of the poor household and would ensure that the girl was married into a wealthy household. Everyone was tenderly taken care of, everyone won in that situation.

Here is another "controversial" passage:

Deuteronomy 21:10 *When thou goest forth to war against thine enemies, and the LORD thy God hath delivered them into thine hands, and thou hast taken them captive,* **11** *And seest among the captives a beautiful woman, and hast a desire unto her, that thou wouldest have her to thy wife;* **12** *Then thou shalt bring her home to thine house; and she shall shave her head, and pare her nails;* **13** *And she shall put the raiment of her captivity from off her, and shall remain in thine house, and bewail her father and her mother a full month: and after that thou shalt go in unto her, and be her husband, and she shall be thy wife.*

The law never did allow for kidnapping people from foreign lands and bringing them back home as slaves. The only thing even remotely close to that, and it is still a long way from it, is what you see here.

In war, the normal operating procedure in those days was to kill everyone. But the law of the Jews allowed for another option. Oftentimes, unless specifically commanded otherwise, captives could be taken. They then became much like serfs in the middle ages. They were not free, but they were not dead, and they were certainly not mistreated. They actually became part of the community.

But in one instance, they could actually become part of the **family.** Some of the ladies from conquered lands were taken as wives. And when they were, they received the exact same rights and kind treatment as any Jewish wife.

Notice that in this passage, the lady who has been taken captive is allowed a month-long period of mourning and adjustment. That was an almost unheard-of act of kindness in the ancient world. And once the wedding was completed, she was not a slave, she was a *wife.*

Here is the last of the "controversial passages." It is one that does delineate one difference between Jewish slaves and foreign slaves:

Leviticus 25:44 *Both thy bondmen, and thy bondmaids, which thou shalt have, shall be of the heathen that are round about you; of them shall ye buy bondmen and bondmaids.* **45** *Moreover of the children of the strangers that do sojourn among you, of them shall ye buy, and of their families that are with you, which they begat in your land: and they shall be your possession.* **46** *And ye shall take them as an inheritance for your children after you, to inherit them for a possession; they shall be your bondmen for ever: but over your brethren the children of Israel, ye shall not rule one over another with rigour.*

Unlike Jewish servants, which were released on year seven, foreign slaves could be purchased and kept forever. But once again, their treatment was far different from the unjust treatment of slavery in the Old South and other places in the more "modern world." They were so loved by God that, if they submitted to circumcision, they were even allowed to participate in the Passover with everyone else:

Exodus 12:44 *But every man's servant that is bought for money, when thou hast circumcised him, then shall he eat thereof.*

It would only be the foreigners who had not been circumcised, so they are to whom this direction is referring. Furthermore, notice that they were not "taken," they were bought, meaning that it was their own people who for whatever reason enslaved them to begin with.

But even more strikingly when you consider it from the spiritual perspective, their "slavery" was the best thing that ever happened to them. Their people sold them out of paganism into the only place on earth where they would come to know the one true God. When you get to heaven, find one and ask him if he is upset about how things worked out! The God of heaven loved him enough to get him to Israel one way or the other, and he will have all eternity to be grateful.

The clinching passages that the critics will not likely ever mention.

Was there servitude in Israel? Yes, there was, along with every other nation on earth at the time. Were they "bought and owned?" Yes:

Leviticus 22:11 *But if the priest **buy any soul** with his money, he shall eat of it, and he that is born in his house: they shall eat of his meat.*

But was it anything like modern slavery? No, in fact, it was not even like the slavery that all of the other nations practiced. Let me show you some things that are absolutely jaw-dropping. One of them we have already seen in another light, but let us look at it again:

Exodus 21:5 *And if the servant shall plainly say, I love my master, my wife, and my children; I will not go out free: 6 Then his master shall bring him unto the judges; he shall also bring him to the door, or unto the door post; and his master shall bore his ear through with an aul; and he shall serve him for ever.*

This is not the picture we would expect. To hear the critics tell it, we would expect a situation where the man loves his wife and children so much that he stays with his hated, abusive master, even though he desperately wants to be free. But did you notice who was at the very front of the list?

"I love *my master*..."

Can you let that sink in? It was expected that every master would treat every servant so well that none of them ever wanted to leave and would instead choose to stay in the master's house forever.

But if that does not clinch it, this surely will, and it is highly likely something you have never heard any critic anywhere point out:

Deuteronomy 23:15 *Thou shalt not deliver unto his master the servant which is escaped from his master unto thee:* **16** *He shall dwell with thee, even among you, in that place which he shall choose in one of thy gates, where it liketh him best: thou shalt not oppress him.*

There should be a major pregnant pause on that one.

Do you understand this? If a servant, slave, whatever you want to call him, ever ran away, no one was to do anything about it. Let him go, period. Why? Here is the implication. Servitude, whether of Jews or foreigners, was to be such a kind, loving thing, that no one would ever even want to leave. If all of the laws that God gave concerning it were followed, then no one would ever have any reason to want to leave! If someone ran, something had to be seriously wrong, because the way God regulated it, no one would want to. Therefore, if a "slave" wanted to go, he could, and everyone was instructed to turn a blind eye to it and to welcome him into their community and let him live with everyone else as a free man.

Does that, does ANY of it, bear any resemblance to "slavery?" No, it does not. And why is that? Here is the answer:

Deuteronomy 16:11 *And thou shalt rejoice before the LORD thy God, thou, and thy son, and thy daughter, and thy manservant, and thy maidservant, and the Levite that is within thy gates, and the stranger, and the fatherless, and the widow, that are among you, in the place which the LORD thy God hath chosen to place his name there.* **12 *And thou shalt remember that thou wast a bondman in Egypt:** and thou shalt observe and do these statutes.*

The children of Israel were treated like slaves for 400 years. Because of that, God never did let them treat anyone else as cruelly oppressed slaves, not for a lifetime, not for a decade, not for a year, not for a month, not for a week, not for a day, not for a minute.

Chapter Five
The Jealousy of God

"The God of the Old Testament is arguably the most unpleasant character in all fiction: jealous and proud of it..."

I have pointed out for four chapters now that critics love to beat on the Old Testament and on the God of the Old Testament. But in this case, it may be more proper to say The Critic rather than simply "critics." By The Critic, I mean the author of the above quote, the foremost source of "wisdom" for all of the other critics on the face of the earth. This man literally is at the very top of their totem pole.

His name is Richard Dawkins.

Dawkins is an avowed atheist and an evolutionary scientist. In 2006 he wrote a book that has become very popular; it is called *The God Delusion*. Little wonder then that scoffers everywhere love to quote him.

Now, let us lay aside the fact that he refers to the Bible as fiction. You and I know better. The Bible has been verified by science, archaeology, and history over and over again. It is that part about the God of the Old Testament being a jealous God that we are interested in for the moment. You see, Dawkins has a lot of Scripture to support his claim that God is a jealous God!

Exodus 20:5 *I the Lord thy God am a jealous God, visiting the iniquity of the fathers upon the children unto the third and fourth generation.*

Exodus 34:14 *For thou shalt worship no other god: for the LORD, whose name is Jealous, is a jealous God:*

Deuteronomy 4:24 *For the LORD thy God is a consuming fire, even a jealous God.*

Deuteronomy 5:9 *I the LORD thy God am a jealous God, visiting the iniquity of the fathers upon the children unto the third and fourth generation.*

Deuteronomy 6:15 *(For the LORD thy God is a jealous God among you) lest the anger of the LORD thy God be kindled against thee, and destroy thee from off the face of the earth.*

Deuteronomy 29:20 *The LORD will not spare him, but then the anger of the LORD and his jealousy shall smoke against that man, and all the curses that are written in this book shall lie upon him, and the LORD shall blot out his name from under heaven.*

Deuteronomy 32:16 *They provoked him to jealousy with strange gods, with abominations provoked they him to anger.*

Deuteronomy 32:21 *They have moved me to jealousy with that which is not God; they have provoked me to anger with their vanities: and I will move them to jealousy with those which are not a people; I will provoke them to anger with a foolish nation.*

Joshua 24:19 *He is a jealous God; he will not forgive your transgressions nor your sins.*

1 Kings 14:22 *And Judah did evil in the sight of the LORD, and they provoked him to jealousy with their sins.*

Ezekiel 8:3 *And he put forth the form of an hand, and took me by a lock of mine head; and the spirit lifted me up between the earth and the heaven, and brought me in the visions of God to Jerusalem, to the door of the inner gate that looketh toward the north; where was the seat of the image of jealousy, which provoketh to jealousy.*

Ezekiel 8:5 *Then said he unto me, Son of man, lift up thine eyes now the way toward the north. So I lifted up mine* *eyes the way toward the north, and behold northward at the gate of the altar this image of jealousy in the entry.*

Ezekiel 16:38 *I will judge thee, as women that break wedlock and shed blood are judged; and I will give thee blood in fury and jealousy.*

Ezekiel 16:42 *So will I make my fury toward thee to rest, and my jealousy shall depart from thee, and I will be quiet, and will be no more angry.*

Ezekiel 23:25 *And I will set my jealousy against thee, and they shall deal furiously with thee: they shall take away thy nose and thine ears; and thy remnant shall fall by the sword: they shall take thy sons and thy daughters; and thy residue shall be devoured by the fire.*

Ezekiel 36:5 *Surely in the fire of my jealousy have I spoken against the residue of the heathen.*

Ezekiel 38:19 *For in my jealousy and in the fire of my wrath have I spoken, Surely in that day there shall be a great shaking in the land of Israel.*

Nahum 1:2 *God is jealous, and the LORD revengeth; the LORD revengeth, and is furious;*

Zechariah 1:14 *Thus saith the LORD of hosts; I am jealous for Jerusalem and for Zion with a great jealousy.*

Zechariah 8:2 *Thus saith the LORD of hosts; I was jealous for Zion with great jealousy, and I was jealous for her with great fury.*

Zephaniah 3:8 *...All the earth shall be devoured with the fire of my jealousy.*

Based on these many verses is it true to say that the God of the Old Testament was or is a jealous God? Absolutely! We agree with Richard Dawkins on that. But that is just about all that we agree on.

So, let us procure our Bibles and our thinking caps as we examine "The Jealousy of God."

The definition of jealousy

When using a word like jealous, one problem we face is that people in the twenty-first century are often lazy. Actually studying something is not nearly as easy as simply assuming, so people choose to assume rather than to study. When the Bible says that God is a jealous God, people automatically begin to form a certain picture in their minds. It is something like an angry redneck boy named Bubba who is mad as fire that Luriene, the girl he likes, is talking to Cletus. And so, in a fit of jealousy, Bubba slashes Cletus' tires on his mud-bog pickup truck.

This is how the critic views God when he is too lazy to study. Jealousy is reduced to some juvenile, immature emotion and is acted upon by being completely unreasonable and destructive. But to be fair and accurate, we should actually find out what the real meaning of the word jealousy is. A very good place to begin would be a dictionary.

The first thing you will notice in any good dictionary is that it is thorough; most every word will have five or six possible meanings under it.

The first thing we find in the Webster's 1828 under the definition of jealousy is "suspicious." That is the very first word. Think of what that means in the human realm.

But is it even possible for God to be "suspicious?" No, and here is why:

Proverbs 15:3 *The eyes of the LORD are in every place, beholding the evil and the good.*

God is omniscient and, therefore, does not have the capacity to ever be suspicious. He actually knows; He never "suspects" anything. So, the very first part of the definition clearly does not and cannot apply to Him. That means that when God is "jealous," it is utterly different than when mankind is jealous. Every ounce of the jealousy of God is always fact-based, never suspicion based.

The second part of the definition is "apprehensive of rivalship." Apprehensive means "fearful." We know that God does not want any rivals for His affection but is it even possible for Him to be "fearful" of a rival or of anything else? No, and here is why:

Revelation 19:6 *And I heard as it were the voice of a great multitude, and as the voice of many waters, and as the voice of mighty thunderings, saying, Alleluia: for the Lord God **omnipotent** reigneth.*

He is omnipotent; He literally has all power.

Revelation 19:15 *And out of his mouth goeth a sharp sword, that with it he should smite the nations: and he shall rule them with a rod of iron: and he treadeth the winepress of the fierceness and wrath of **Almighty** God.*

He is almighty, unrivaled in might. It is not in the capacity of God to be apprehensive about anything. Therefore the second part of the definition clearly does not apply to Him.

Another part of the definition we see here is the word "uneasy" which also clearly cannot apply to an omnipotent, almighty God.

These make up the vast bulk of the descriptions and definitions of the word "jealousy," and they clearly do not apply to God. But there are two that do apply to Him:

"Solicitous to defend the honor of."

"Anxiously careful and concerned for."

Those two definitions work quite nicely with what we see in Scripture no matter which way we take them, and I believe logic dictates that on the first one, we take it both ways. God is very clearly solicitous to defend honor, both His and ours. He does not want anyone dishonoring Him:

Isaiah 48:11 *For mine own sake, even for mine own sake, will I do it: for how should my name be polluted? and **I will not give my glory unto another.***

He also does not want anyone, including us, dishonoring us.

Ezekiel 36:5 *Therefore thus saith the Lord GOD; Surely in the fire of my jealousy have I spoken against the* *residue of the heathen, and against all Idumea, which have appointed my land into their possession with the joy of all their heart, with despiteful minds, to cast it out for a prey. 6 Prophesy therefore concerning the land of Israel, and say unto the mountains, and to the hills, to the rivers, and to the valleys, Thus saith the Lord GOD; Behold, I have spoken in my jealousy and in my fury, because ye have borne the shame of the heathen: 7 Therefore thus saith the Lord GOD; I have lifted up mine hand, Surely the heathen that are about you, they shall bear their shame. 8 But ye, O mountains of Israel, ye shall shoot forth your branches, and yield your fruit to my people of Israel; for they are at hand to come. 9 For, behold, I am for you, and I will turn unto you, and ye shall be tilled and sown:*

Now please think through those two things. First of all, is it right of God to be jealous of His own glory and not want to give it to another? Let us try a "what if" scenario. What if you secured a copy of "The God Delusion" or "The Blind Watchmaker" or any of the other sixty-six books that Richard Dawkins has written. What if you then made copies of them, put your name on the cover, and started selling them?

It would not take long at all for you to be hit with a massive lawsuit. But why? Isn't jealousy a bad thing? Isn't God a terrible ogre for being jealous of His own glory? Why then would Richard Dawkins be jealous of his glory? Unless, of course, jealousy is not always a bad thing.

There is nothing wrong or inappropriate at all for the Creator to be jealous of the glory of His creation. The fact of the matter is, if there is anyone that can never be wrong by being jealous over His glory, it is God. But He is also jealous over ours. He made us, He loves us, and He wants us to retain the glory of purity and righteousness. Every time He spoke of jealousy to Israel, it was always in reference to them debasing themselves to the level of the filthy idolatrous heathens around them:

Exodus 32:25 *And when Moses saw that the people were naked; (for Aaron had made them naked unto their **shame** among their enemies:)*

Yes, God was jealous over that kind of thing; He was jealous for the glory of His people! Why does a good father not let his daughter out of the house dressed immodestly? He is jealous over her glory. Why does a good mother not let her son near some promiscuous girl? She is jealous over his glory. I for one am very glad that God is jealous, not just over His glory, but over mine as well!

The second part of the definition that actually applies to God is "anxiously careful and concerned for."

When it comes to God, clearly this one does not apply from Him to Him. God is not concerned for anything about Himself; He is the God who has always been and will always be. But He is most definitely careful and concerned for us. Dawkins and His acolytes love to point out all of the verses that say that God was jealous and was going to punish Israel. But let me show you what they do not have nearly as much use for:

Jeremiah 31:3 *The LORD hath appeared of old unto me, saying, Yea, I have loved thee with an everlasting love: therefore with lovingkindness have I drawn thee.*

Deuteronomy 33:27a *The eternal God is thy refuge, and underneath are the everlasting arms:*

Deuteronomy 23:5 *Nevertheless the LORD thy God would not hearken unto Balaam; but the LORD thy God turned the curse into a blessing unto thee, because the LORD thy God loved thee.*

Isaiah 43:4a *Since thou wast precious in my sight, thou hast been honourable, and I have loved thee:*

I could give you hundreds of more verses of this sort. God loved His people fiercely. He was anxiously, carefully concerned for them.

He brought them into Egypt to survive the famine.

He brought them out of Egypt to free them from slavery.

He parted the Red Sea and then collapsed it to rid them of Pharaoh.

He sent them angel food from heaven for forty years.

He gave them a kingdom.

God loved His people, and He was very good to them. His jealousy was for their benefit, it was never arbitrary or capricious, and it was always fact-based, never suspicion based.

The delight of jealousy

I know that is a phrase you may never have heard or read and may never hear or read again. But I want you to think your way through it because, in the case of God, it makes perfect sense.

Zechariah 8:2 *Thus saith the LORD of hosts; I was jealous for Zion with great jealousy, and I was jealous for her with great fury.*

Are you married? How many of you would have married your spouse if he or she had at the very beginning said this:

"Look, we may be getting married, but don't expect me to care what you do or who you are with, and don't expect me to pay any attention to you if you decide to care what I do or who I am with. You want to sleep around? Knock yourself out, because I am most definitely going to do the same thing..."

There are, no doubt, in this present wicked age a few people who would claim to hold that view. A very few, not many at all. But the funny thing is, I actually remember a famous actress who did. She once famously proclaimed, "monogamy is a man-made invention." And then a tragic thing happened; her husband met another woman. The last news story I saw said that she is "learning to forgive him for what he did."

Learning to forgive what? I thought monogamy was a man-made invention, and that people were not supposed to care about things like faithfulness?

No one in their right mind feels that way. It is instinctively understood that jealousy is a part of love and that without jealousy there really is no love. In other words, the more people love each other, the more angry and hurt they would be if adultery took place.

If you want to know if a man has the capacity for jealousy, you could perhaps try something incredibly stupid such as flirting with his wife. But you may want to make sure your medical insurance is paid up before you do because jealousy is a vital part of love. And yet, do you realize how incredibly impressive it is that God is jealous over His relationship with us? Why should He be? That is akin to a super-model being jealous over a relationship with the world's ugliest, smelliest man. God, in all of His purity and holiness and perfection, is jealous over His relationship with us! That is not something I cringe at; it is something I delight in.

Chapter Six
The Treatment of Women

Here is a list of claims someone made me aware of, ripping into God's "horrible treatment of women:"

"Women's behavior (in the Bible) was extremely limited in ancient times, much as the women of Afghanistan during the recent Taliban oppression. For instance:

"Unmarried women could not leave the home of their father without permission.

"Married women had to get permission from their husbands to step out of the home.

"Women were restricted to roles of little or no authority.

"Women could not testify in court.

"Women could not appear in public places.

"Women could not talk to strangers.

"Women had to wear a double veil when they left their homes."

Let us examine the accusations. Number one was "Unmarried women could not leave the home of their father without permission."

To begin with, even if that were entirely true, how in the world would it be a terrible thing? Any child still living at home ought to be subject to their parents, and if they are too big to be subject to their parents, they are too big to live at home.

But as you study the Old Testament, you find that, far from being a "girl thing," it was actually an "everybody thing." Jesse told his adult children, all boys, where and when they could come and go. It was the same with Jacob and his adult sons. In fact, in the case of Jacob as we read about him refusing to allow Benjamin to leave home and then about him sending his sons into Egypt, he was dealing with sons that were full grown adults with children of their own and nearing what in our day would be considered "retirement age." In the Bible days, as long as you were living at home, daddy called the shots, and it did not matter whether you were a boy or a girl or a man or a woman.

The second claim was, "Married women had to get permission from their husbands to step out of the home." Those who know their Bibles are probably already aware of the fact that there is no law or commandment that says this. But what we do find is an example of a woman whom her husband wanted to stay home, and she would not:

Proverbs 7:1 *My son, keep my words, and lay up my commandments with thee.* **2** *Keep my commandments, and live; and my law as the apple of thine eye.* **3** *Bind them upon thy fingers, write them upon the table of thine heart.* **4** *Say unto wisdom, Thou art my sister; and call understanding thy kinswoman:* **5** *That they may keep thee from the strange woman, from the stranger which flattereth with her words.* **6** *For at the window of my house I looked through my casement,* **7** *And beheld among the simple ones, I discerned among the youths, a young man void of understanding,* **8** *Passing through the street near her corner; and he went the way to her house,* **9** *In the twilight, in the evening, in the black and dark night:* **10** *And, behold, there met him a woman with the attire of an harlot, and subtil of heart.* **11** *(She is loud and stubborn; her feet abide not in her house:* **12** *Now is she without, now in the streets, and lieth in wait at every corner.)* **13** *So she caught him, and kissed him, and with an impudent face said unto him,* **14** *I have peace offerings with* *me; this day have I payed my vows.* **15** *Therefore came I forth to meet thee, diligently to seek thy face, and I have found thee.* **16** *I have decked my bed with coverings of tapestry, with carved works, with fine linen of Egypt.* **17** *I have perfumed my bed with myrrh, aloes, and cinnamon.* **18** *Come, let us take our fill of love until the morning: let us solace ourselves with loves.* **19** *For the goodman is not at home, he is gone a long journey:* **20** *He hath taken a bag of money with him, and will come home at the day appointed.* **21** *With her much fair speech she caused him to yield, with the flattering of her lips she forced him.* **22** *He goeth after her straightway, as an ox goeth to the slaughter, or as a fool to the correction of the stocks;* **23** *Till a dart strike through his liver; as a bird hasteth to the snare, and knoweth not that it is for his life.*

This woman would be held up by the critics and the modern world as a good example of a liberated woman, a good example of how things ought to be. But did you happen to notice that she violated her own marriage and ruined several other young men in the process? The fact is, when a man and a woman get married, they are both supposed to "stay home," and neither ought to go anywhere without the other party being privy to it and comfortable with it.

The third claim was, "Women were restricted to roles of little or no authority." That one, to me, is the most hilarious one of all:

In Judges 4 and 5, Deborah is described as both a Judge of Israel and as the leader in the army. Big bad Barak would not even go to war unless she came along. And the story ends with another amazing woman, Jael, killing the enemy and receiving the accolades for it.

Now look at this:

2 Kings 22:6 *Unto carpenters, and builders, and masons, and to buy timber and hewn stone to repair the house.* **7** *Howbeit there was no reckoning made with them of the money that was delivered into their hand, because they dealt faithfully.* **8** *And Hilkiah the high priest said unto*

Shaphan the scribe, I have found the book of the law in the house of the LORD. And Hilkiah gave the book to Shaphan, and he read it. **9** *And Shaphan the scribe came to the king, and brought the king word again, and said, Thy servants have gathered the money that was found in the house, and have delivered it into the hand of them that do the work, that have the oversight of the house of the LORD.* **10** *And Shaphan the scribe shewed the king, saying, Hilkiah the priest hath delivered me a book. And Shaphan read it before the king.* **11** *And it came to pass, when the king had heard the words of the book of the law, that he rent his clothes.* **12** *And the king commanded Hilkiah the priest, and Ahikam the son of Shaphan, and Achbor the son of Michaiah, and Shaphan the scribe, and Asahiah a servant of the king's, saying,* **13** *Go ye, enquire of the LORD for me, and for the people, and for all Judah, concerning the words of this book that is found: for great is the wrath of the LORD that is kindled against us, because our fathers have not hearkened unto the words of this book, to do according unto all that which is written concerning us.* **14** *So Hilkiah the priest, and Ahikam, and Achbor, and Shaphan, and Asahiah,* ***went unto Huldah the prophetess****, the wife of Shallum the son of Tikvah, the son of Harhas, keeper of the wardrobe; (now she dwelt in Jerusalem in the college;)* ***and they communed with her.***

In this particular instance, when the people needed an answer from God, they went to a woman, Huldah, the prophetess. Do you know what makes that so impressive? This was during the time of Jeremiah and Zephaniah, but they were not even consulted!

We can also find at least three other female prophets, including Miriam, Noadiah, and Isaiah's wife.

And then there was this lady named Esther, Queen Esther, maybe you have heard of her.

There was also this other lady who had a Bible book named after her; her name was Ruth.

The fourth claim was that they "could not testify in court." Do please let me know if you ever find a Bible verse that says that because it simply is not there. If men ever behaved in that manner, they did so without God directing them to do so.

The fifth claim was that "Women could not appear in public places." Well, that is interesting. Not only does the Bible not actually say that, but it actually does say this:

2 Samuel 6:18 *And as soon as David had made an end of offering burnt offerings and peace offerings, he blessed the people in the name of the LORD of hosts.* **19** *And he dealt among all the people, even among the whole multitude of Israel, as well to the women as men, to every one a cake of bread, and a good piece of flesh, and a flagon of wine. So all the people departed every one to his house.*

Quite simply, despite the protestations of the critics, this passage shows us all of the women of the nation appearing in a public venue. Here is another one:

1 Samuel 18:6 *And it came to pass as they came, when David was returned from the slaughter of the Philistine, that the women came out of all cities of Israel, singing and dancing, to meet king Saul, with tabrets, with joy, and with instruments of musick.* **7** *And the women answered one another as they played, and said, Saul hath slain his thousands, and David his ten thousands.*

Here is another one:

Exodus 15:20 *And Miriam the prophetess, the sister of Aaron, took a timbrel in her hand; and all the women went out after her with timbrels and with dances.* **21** *And Miriam answered them, Sing ye to the LORD, for he hath triumphed gloriously; the horse and his rider hath he thrown into the sea.*

Here is another one:

Proverbs 31:16 *She considereth a field, and buyeth it: with the fruit of her hands she planteth a vineyard.*

73

You are going to be hard-pressed to find many books of the Old Testament where there were not a whole bunch of women appearing in public venues.

The next accusation was "Women could not talk to strangers." Once again, the problem is, the Bible never says that. Look at this:

Judges 13:6 *Then the woman came and told her husband, saying, A man of God came unto me, and his countenance was like the countenance of an angel of God, very terrible: but I asked him not whence he was, neither told he me his name: 7 But he said unto me, Behold, thou shalt conceive, and bear a son; and now drink no wine nor strong drink, neither eat any unclean thing: for the child shall be a Nazarite to God from the womb to the day of his death.*

Here is another one:

1 Samuel 25:18 *Then Abigail made haste, and took two hundred loaves, and two bottles of wine, and five sheep ready dressed, and five measures of parched corn, and an hundred clusters of raisins, and two hundred cakes of figs, and laid them on asses. 19 And she said unto her servants, Go on before me; behold, I come after you. But she told not her husband Nabal. 20 And it was so, as she rode on the ass, that she came down by the covert of the hill, and, behold, David and his men came down against her; and she met them. 21 Now David had said, Surely in vain have I kept all that this fellow hath in the wilderness, so that nothing was missed of all that pertained unto him: and he hath requited me evil for good. 22 So and more also do God unto the enemies of David, if I leave of all that pertain to him by the morning light any that pisseth against the wall. 23 And when Abigail saw David, she hasted, and lighted off the ass, and fell before David on her face, and bowed herself to the ground, 24 And fell at his feet, and said, Upon me, my lord, upon me let this iniquity be: and let thine handmaid, I pray thee, speak in thine audience, and hear the words of thine handmaid.*

There are many more examples of this as well.

The last accusation is "Women had to wear a double veil when they left their homes." That is very interesting. The word "veil" appears in the Old Testament with that spelling just once, and it has nothing to do with a command of any kind:

Song of Solomon 5:7 *The watchmen that went about the city found me, they smote me, they wounded me; the keepers of the walls took away my veil from me.*

It is also spelled as vail, and in that case, it occurs a few more times. But of those times with that spelling, it most often refers not to something that a person wore, but to the thick curtain in the holy of holies. Let me give you the list of verses where it applies to a person, and I think you will be very surprised by a few things.

Genesis 24:65 *For she had said unto the servant, What man is this that walketh in the field to meet us? And the servant had said, It is my master: therefore she took a vail, and covered herself.*

Genesis 38:14 *And she put her widow's garments off from her, and covered her with a vail, and wrapped herself, and sat in an open place, which is by the way to Timnath; for she saw that Shelah was grown, and she was not given unto him to wife.*

Genesis 38:19 *And she arose, and went away, and laid by her vail from her, and put on the garments of her widowhood.*

Exodus 34:34 *But when Moses went in before the LORD to speak with him, he took the vail off, until he came out. And he came out, and spake unto the children of Israel that which he was commanded.*

Exodus 34:35 *And the children of Israel saw the face of Moses, that the skin of Moses' face shone: and Moses put the vail upon his face again, until he went in to speak with him.*

Ruth 3:15 *Also he said, Bring the vail that thou hast upon thee, and hold it. And when she held it, he measured six* *measures of barley, and laid it on her: and she went into the city.*

In the entire Old Testament, this is it. These are the only times the word veil is mentioned by either spelling in reference to something people wore. And in no verse does it say anything about "double veiled." Double veiled is not mentioned in the Bible anywhere. And, to make matters more interesting, not everyone in the Old Testament even regarded a veil as a sign of modesty. In fact, it often meant something very, very different. Take the case of Tamar that we saw a few verses ago:

Genesis 38:15 *When Judah saw her, he thought her to be an harlot; because she had covered her face.*

So, to recap, God never commanded a woman to veil her face, some women did veil their faces because they believed it made them more modest, some wore veils because they thought it identified them as being for hire, but nowhere is a double veil even mentioned, let alone commanded.

Furthermore, did you happen to notice that on occasion, even men wore them? In two different verses, we actually saw Moses in a veil.

Moving on, there are a couple of chapters in the Old Testament that the critics love to hate, Exodus 20-21. They call them "The two most misogynistic chapters in the Bible." That word means "reflecting or exhibiting hatred, dislike, mistrust, or mistreatment of women."

That is a serious accusation. And why do they view Exodus 20-21 like that? The letter I received said,

"Exodus 20:17 lists the last of the Ten Commandments: 'Thou shalt not covet thy neighbor's house, thou shalt not covet thy neighbor's wife, nor his manservant, nor his maidservant, nor his ox, nor his ass, nor anything that is thy neighbor's.'

"The tenth commandment forbids coveting your neighbor's house, wife, male slave, female slave, animals or anything else that the neighbor owns. The wife is clearly regarded as equivalent to a piece of property."

What? I have read my Bible through about fifty times, and it has never once dawned on me to view that commandment that way. How many of you men want some other man wanting your wife? No?

Well then, according to these people, you view her as a piece of property. Logically then, by contrast, the only way to not view her as a piece of property is to be okay with other men wanting her.

Do you see how ridiculous that is? The fact is, God simply listed the things that men were likely to covet and told them not to. Some of it was property, but not all of it. One thing men would be prone to covet is a person, someone else's wife. That is all this commandment says.

Study your Bible, and here is what you will find. Far from God expecting that women be viewed as property, we find that Eve was part of the special creation of God, along with Adam, and God walked and talked with both of them. She was a "helpmeet," which means a counterpart, an opposite to complete the man, which means that he is incomplete without her.

We also find:

Ephesians 5:25 *Husbands, love your wives, even as Christ also loved the church, and gave himself for it;*

Yes, I know that is the New Testament, but it is the view of God all the way through Scripture. Property?

Proverbs 18:22 *Whoso findeth a wife findeth a good thing, and obtaineth favour of the LORD.*

Property?

Genesis 24:67 *And Isaac brought her into his mother Sarah's tent, and took Rebekah, and she became his wife; and* **he loved her***: and Isaac was comforted after his mother's death*

Property?

1 Samuel 1:5 *But unto Hannah he gave a worthy portion; for he loved Hannah:*

Read the Song of Solomon and tell me if that girl was regarded as property or as the love of a man's life. Read the book of Ruth and tell me if that girl was regarded as property or as the love of a man's life. Read Proverbs 31 and tell me if that girl was regarded as property or as the love of a man's life.

Were there men in the Old Testament who treated women like dogs or worse? Yes, some did. But did they do so because of Scripture or in spite of it? In spite of it. Were there polygamists? Yes. But was that God's plan? No:

Genesis 2:24 *Therefore shall a man leave his father and his mother, and shall cleave unto his wife: and they shall be one flesh.*

Another attack against God in relation to women was sent to me as follows:

"The first seventeen verses of Exodus 22 deal with restitution in case of stealing, or damage to, a person's property. Verses sixteen and seventeen deal with the case of a man who seduces a virgin. This was viewed as a property offense against the woman's father. The woman was expected to marry the seducer. If her father refused to transfer ownership of his daughter to the seducer, the latter was required to pay money to her father. The money would be in compensation for the damage to the father's property - his daughter. It would be difficult for a non-virgin to marry."

Really. Let's look at it:

Exodus 22:16 *And if a man entice a maid that is not betrothed, and lie with her, he shall surely endow her to be his wife.* **17** *If her father utterly refuse to give her unto him, he shall pay money according to the dowry of virgins.*

Please notice that the word "property" does not occur anywhere. Notice as well that no rape has occurred; the situation is one in which a guy has convinced a girl to sleep with him. In other words, they have both sinned. And, while today that might not seem like a huge deal even though it is, back then everyone knew it was a huge deal. And back then people were expected to take responsibility for what they did. In this case, no guy was allowed to seduce a girl and then simply move on to the next conquest. If you got a girl to sleep with you, you better be ready to marry her, because if she wanted to marry you and the father wanted her to marry you, you as the man had no right to say no.

Please tell me again how God and the Old Testament is "anti-woman?" If anything, this sounds a whole lot like "anti-man." But what if the guy was a loser, and the father knew it? Then he could refuse to allow there to be a marriage but could instead hit the guy in his pocketbook for what he did.

Once again, how is that anti-woman? The only person in the entire passage that is getting hammered on, the only person in the entire passage who has no say in how things go whatsoever is the man.

Here was the next accusation I was accosted with:

"Exodus 21:22-25 describes a situation in which two men are fighting, and one hits a pregnant woman. If the woman has a miscarriage because of the blow, the man is punished as the husband decides and must pay a fine for their act - not to the woman, but to her husband, presumably because he has been deprived of a child. The woman had no involvement. Exodus 21:22: '...he shall be surely punished, according as the woman's husband will lay upon him; and he shall pay as the judges determine.'"

Once again, let us actually look at the passage:

Exodus 21:22 *If men strive, and hurt a woman with child, so that her fruit depart from her, and yet no mischief follow: he shall be surely punished, according as the woman's husband will lay upon him; and he shall pay as the judges determine. 23 And if any mischief follow, then thou shalt give life for life, 24 Eye for eye, tooth for tooth, hand for hand,* *foot for foot,* **25** *Burning for burning, wound for wound, stripe for stripe.*

Let us begin by correcting the incredibly poor excuse for scholarship of the scoffers. They said "Exodus 21:22-25 describes a situation in which two men are fighting, and one hits a pregnant woman. If the woman has a miscarriage because of the blow, the man is punished." But please listen very carefully. The Bible does not say or mean miscarriage. It says "so that her fruit depart from her, and yet no mischief follow..."

That means that, after getting hit during the fight, the woman went into labor and gave birth. Her fruit "departed from her," the baby came out. But then it says "...and yet no mischief follow..." that means that the baby lived. She gave birth because of getting hit when the two guys were fighting, she went into labor, but the baby lived. In that case, the man who hit her and caused her to go into labor is still punished; he has to pay monetary restitution, because after all, there will probably be some medical expenses incurred for her and the baby.

How again is that anti-woman? In fact, how is it even significantly different from our own code of law today? In the exact same situation, much the same thing would be done by our modern law. But then we read:

Exodus 21:23 *And if any mischief follow, then thou shalt give life for life, Eye for eye, tooth for tooth, hand for hand, foot for foot,* **24** *Burning for burning, wound for wound, stripe for stripe.*

In other words, if the baby or the woman dies or is injured, the man who did it is either killed or injured to the same degree. This is not anti-woman, the only one getting punished is the man.

Here is another one of the accusations I received:

"Exodus 23:17 tells us that only men are required to take part in the three big feasts for Israel: 'Three times in the year all thy males shall appear before the Lord GOD.'"

I love this, I just love this. If women were "required" to go to Jerusalem three times a year and worship, imagine the howls of protests; "God is so mean! How dare he make women go all the way to Jerusalem three times a year!" But because He did not require it, because He laid a **requirement** on the men, somehow, He is still anti-woman. Women were **allowed and encouraged** to go to all of those feasts, and they usually did. But they did not **have to.** Only the men **had to.** So, therefore, God is clearly anti-woman.

What utter drivel.

Here is another accusation:

"Women were not allowed to become priests."

That is correct, they were not. But apparently, even though they could be prophetesses, judges over the entire nation, and queens, God is somehow anti-woman in this. No, He has the right to set limits on all of us, and He has. And what these critics cannot seem to grasp is that not only were women not allowed to be priests, but 99.99 percent of the **men** were not allowed to be priests either.

No one who was not from the tribe of Levi could be a priest, that eliminated 12/13th of the male population, or 92.3 percent. But then we read in Numbers 16:40 that even most of the tribe of Levi could not be a priest, only those descended from Aaron and his sons could do that. That even left out Moses and his descendants! Then we read this:

Numbers 4:3 *From thirty years old and upward even until fifty years old, all that enter into the host, to do the work in the tabernacle of the congregation.*

This tells us that no one under thirty or over fifty could be a priest in the tabernacle of the congregation. That left out a large percentage of other men. Then we find this:

Leviticus 21:16 *And the LORD spake unto Moses, saying,* **17** *Speak unto Aaron, saying, Whosoever he be of thy seed in their generations that hath any blemish, let him not approach to offer the bread of his God.* **18** *For whatsoever man he be that hath a blemish, he shall not approach: a blind* *man, or a lame, or he that hath a flat nose, or any thing superfluous,* **19** *Or a man that is brokenfooted, or brokenhanded,* **20** *Or crookbackt, or a dwarf, or that hath a blemish in his eye, or be scurvy, or scabbed, or hath his stones broken;* **21** *No man that hath a blemish of the seed of Aaron the priest shall come nigh to offer the offerings of the LORD made by fire: he hath a blemish; he shall not come nigh to offer the bread of his God.* **22** *He shall eat the bread of his God, both of the most holy, and of the holy.* **23** *Only he shall not go in unto the vail, nor come nigh unto the altar, because he hath a blemish; that he profane not my sanctuaries: for I the LORD do sanctify them.* **24** *And Moses told it unto Aaron, and to his sons, and unto all the children of Israel.*

That prohibited a great deal more. Thus, one hundred percent of women could not be a priest, but 99.99 percent of men could not be a priest either! So how exactly is that anti-woman? What was God doing? He was using the Old Testament priesthood to point to our Great High Priest, the **man** Christ Jesus:

1 Timothy 2:5 *For there is one God, and one mediator between God and men,* ***the man*** *Christ Jesus;*

Here is another of the accusations given to me:

"Numbers 5:11-31 describes a magical ritual that women were forced to perform if their husbands suspected them of cheating. A priest prepared a magic potion and then proclaimed a curse over the potion and required the woman to drink it. If she were guilty, she would suffer greatly: her abdomen would swell, and her thighs waste away. There is no similar magical test for husbands suspecting of having an affair with another woman."

Magic? Magic had nothing to do with it. This was the power and the knowledge of God, it was heavenly science, and it worked every single time. And it was not just a foolproof way to determine if a woman was guilty, it was also a foolproof way to determine if she was innocent, because if she was innocent, nothing at all happened. Do you realize that makes them thousands of years ahead of us even though they were thousands of years behind us? Who would not rather have that option available today than what we currently have, which is years of suspicion and jealousy and hatred?

But what about the no similar test for men? Correct. All God did with the men was what He did with David, the sword never departing from his house because of his adultery, and with Samson, who lost his eyes and his life for his sexual sin.

So how again is this anti-woman?

In going through passages that the skeptics point at to try and prove their pre-determined conclusions, you will find that there are some that they stay as far away from as they can because they completely torpedo their falsehoods. Here is a passage these folks do not usually bother to mention:

Deuteronomy 22:25 *But if a man find a betrothed damsel in the field, and the man force her, and lie with her: then the man only that lay with her shall die:* **26** *But unto the damsel thou shalt do nothing; there is in the damsel no sin worthy of death: for as when a man riseth against his neighbour, and slayeth him, even so is this matter:* **27** *For he found her in the field, and the betrothed damsel cried, and there was none to save her.*

Do you remember the equation that was made earlier, that the treatment of women in the Old Testament was much the same as the treatment of women under the Taliban? Think, if you have been watching the news for the past twelve years or so, if a woman is raped under the Taliban, who is it that gets stoned? The victim. The woman. But God's law laid out just the opposite approach, the right approach. The woman was regarded as innocent, she lived, nothing was done to her, and the man, the rapist, was put to death.

Were women expected to obey their fathers and then their husbands? Yes. They still are. But were men ever allowed to be ogres or jerks or view their wives as property?

83

No, not by God at least. By their culture maybe, by their traditions maybe, but not by God and not by Scripture, Old Testament or otherwise. Men were and are commanded to love their wives **as** Christ loved the church and **gave Himself** for it.

Did men divorce their wives, often for little or no reason? Yes. But was God in favor of that? No:

Malachi 2:14 *Yet ye say, Wherefore? Because the LORD hath been witness between thee and the wife of thy youth, against whom thou hast dealt treacherously: yet is she thy companion, and the wife of thy covenant.* **15** *And did not he make one? Yet had he the residue of the spirit. And wherefore one? That he might seek a godly seed. Therefore take heed to your spirit, and let none deal treacherously against the wife of his youth.* **16** *For the LORD, the God of Israel, saith that he hateth putting away: for one covereth violence with his garment, saith the LORD of hosts: therefore take heed to your spirit, that ye deal not treacherously.*

Matthew 19:8 *He saith unto them, Moses because of the hardness of your hearts suffered you to put away your wives: but from the beginning it was not so.*

Did some men view their wives as weak and worthless? Yes. But was that God's idea? No. In fact, men who walked with God showed a very different example:

Aquilla and Priscilla worked for God together and taught Apollos together.

The Proverbs 31 woman was both a submissive wife and a liberated dynamo at the same time.

Here is another thing that critics just love to blister the Bible with. The Bible, they say, is anti-woman because if you look at the temple, there was a court of women, but then there were places past the court of women that only the men could go. Men were therefore regarded as being better than women.

That is very interesting. Let me ask a question, and you see if you can come up with the right numerical answer. How many times does the phrase "the Court of Women" appear in the Bible? The answer is, a huge, whopping, none. Not one single time does that phrase appear in Scripture. The nearest thing you will find in Scripture is "the court of the women's house" in Esther 2:11, which referred not to the Jewish temple but to the Persian palace.

Was there such a place as the Court of Women? Yes, there was, it was present at least in Herod's Temple, the third of the Jewish temples. Solomon's was first, then Zerubbabel's, then Herod's. And it is in that third temple, built by Herod, that we first become acquainted with the Court of Women.

God Himself gave the pattern for the tabernacle in the wilderness. But there are no specific instructions given in Scripture as to the layout of the temple, except for the Holy Place and the Holy of Holies, which were nothing more than the tabernacle brought indoors.

The courtyard system of Herod's temple was as follows. The very outer layer was the court of the Gentiles. If you were a Gentile, it did not matter if you were a man or woman, that was as far as you could go.

The second layer was the women's court. Only Jews could come into it, and Jewish ladies were welcomed into it. Past that was the court of Israel. Only Jewish men were allowed there. Past that was the court of the priests, only Jewish men who were descended from Aaron and in the priesthood could go that far. Past that was the Holy Place, only certain of the priests could go into that, and past that was the Holy of Holies, and only the high priest could go into that, and he could only go once a year.

Please understand that everything outside of the Holy Place and Holy of Holies, all of those courtyards, you will not find any of that specified or commanded in Scripture. The nearest that you will find were some restrictions placed on Gentiles, man or woman.

Furthermore, here is what the critics either do not know or will not willingly tell you:

The International Standard Bible Encyclopedia says, "The eastern gate, approached from the outside by twelve steps, admitted into the court of the women, so called because it was accessible to women as well as to men. **Above its single colonnades were galleries reserved for the use of women**." In other words, there were places in the temple that women could not go, *but there were also places in the temple that men could not go!* (5:2938)

Is the Bible, Old or New Testament, anti-woman?

Eve sinned first, yet the hammer of judgment fell on Adam not on Eve.

When Jesus came to earth, He had an earthly mother but not an earthly Father.

There are five ladies specifically highlighted in the line of Christ.

Rahab, the former prostitute, is in the Hebrews 11 "Hall of Faith" as is Sarah.

Two books of the Bible are named for women.

If a man refused to become a kinsman redeemer to a woman, Deuteronomy 25:9 tells us that she, a woman, was *allowed to spit in his face!*

When the daughters of Zelophehad came before Moses and the congregation in Numbers 27 with a complaint and request, Moses publicly said, *"The daughters of Zelophehad speak right: thou shalt surely give them a possession of an inheritance among their father's brethren; and thou shalt cause the inheritance of their father to pass unto them."* Under the law, as they knew it, their inheritance could have been given to men. But God through Moses said no, ruling in favor of these girls.

As you read the law, does it sometimes sound very strict toward women? Yes. But it also sounds very strict toward men. Everyone under the law felt like they were "in bondage," men and women. But there was a purpose for it:

Galatians 3:24 *Wherefore the law was our schoolmaster to bring us unto Christ, that we might be justified by faith.*

Everything strict toward women and strict toward men in the Old Testament was designed to show us our need for a Savior! But even that Old Testament strictness is now gone, both for men and women:

Romans 6:14 *For sin shall not have dominion over you: for ye are not under the law, but under grace.*

Anti-woman? Not the Bible, not at all. In fact, most of the terrible things we hear that supposedly happened to women usually happened only to men! The critic's quote that I gave you at the beginning of this chapter said that things in Bible times were terrible for women, just like under the Taliban in Afghanistan. But let me pose a question. Not just under the Taliban, but under Islam everywhere, who is it that is constantly getting stoned to death even right now in the "enlightened" 21st century? Women, always women, it never seems to happen to the men. And supposedly, the Bible treatment of women was like the Taliban treatment of women.

So here is a follow-up question. In the Bible, how many accounts are there of people being stoned to death?

The answer is seven, just seven. And in how many of those accounts were women stoned to death? The answer is one, one out of seven. In all seven cases, a man was stoned to death, in exactly one of those cases was a woman stoned to death. Seven to one!

The Old Testament times were not warm and cuddly; they were hard and strict. But they were most definitely not anti-woman, and God was not and is not anti-woman, and the Bible was not and is not anti-woman, not even the Old Testament.

Chapter Seven
The God Who Kills

When you listen to the critics of Scripture, you will find that they love to accuse God of the most horrific things:

> "The God of the Old Testament is arguably the most unpleasant character in all fiction: jealous and proud of it; a petty, unjust, unforgiving control-freak; a vindictive, bloodthirsty ethnic cleanser; a misogynistic, homophobic, racist, infanticidal, genocidal, filicidal, pestilential, megalomaniacal, sadomasochistic, capriciously malevolent bully." Richard Dawkins in *The God Delusion*.

Among other things, Richard Dawkins wants you to not believe in God because, according to him, God is "a bloodthirsty ethnic cleanser, infanticidal, genocidal, and filicidal." God is a serial killer, in other words.

When things like this are thrown around you can be certain of a few things. One, some people will never check to see if they are either false or greatly overstated, they will simply believe it because they do not want to believe in God anyway. Two, you can be certain that many of the people making vicious claims against God are the biggest hypocrites on the planet.

I want us to look at our Old Testament and find out that we do not need to fear it, not even in this. We will begin, though, by showing you just how incredibly hypocritical the skeptics of Scripture are. You see, these supposedly kind, ethical, moral people who are horrified at all of the meanness of God, are not at all what they seem. They want you to believe that they are simply horrified at a God who would kill children and that they cannot believe that you would believe anything that such a horrible God says. But we would do well to examine the character of the people making those hateful claims against God.

An examination of the skeptics

"There is not enough space to mention all the places in the Bible where God committed, commanded or condoned murder." Dan Barker (*Godless,* 177)

Dan Barker (born June 25, 1949) is an American atheist activist who served as a Christian preacher and musician for nineteen years but left Christianity in 1984. He, along with his wife Annie Laurie Gaylor, is the current co-president of the Freedom From Religion Foundation. These are the folks that constantly file lawsuits against anything that offends their non-religious sensibilities, things like nativity scenes and prayers at ball games.

Barker wrote a popular book called *Godless.* Dan Barker despises the God he claims not to believe in, especially the God of the Old Testament. And, when debating with people who do believe in God, he absolutely loves to make God out to be a murderer, as in the quote I gave you from him just a moment ago. According to Dan Barker, the so-called "God killings" of the Old Testament mean that you should either hate Him or at least not believe in Him.

But you see, the thing about getting rid of God is that in so doing, you leave yourself with no absolute moral standard to go by. Dan Barker actually admits that. In a debate with Peter Payne at the University of Wisconsin in March of 2005, he said, "There are no actions in and of themselves that are always absolutely right or wrong. It depends on the context. You cannot name an action that is always absolutely right or wrong. I can think of an exception in any case." (Barker Debate)

In other words, he believes it could be right to rape one, two, or even two million little girls, to torture babies, to gouge out the eyes of children, and yet he is for some reason upset with God for killing!

Do you see the hypocrisy and inconsistency? What it boils down to is that he and brilliant skeptics like him have the right to decide to rape and torture and kill under certain circumstances, but God is wrong every time He brings about a death. But if there is no absolute right or absolute wrong then Dan Barker and critics like him can only be consistent by admitting that it is possible that God was right each and every time He killed.

When faced with that, here is how he responded. Barker said, "OK I admit that. But the children? The fetuses?" In other words, he first of all says that there could be circumstances under which it is right to kill children, and then he gets upset with God for bringing about the death of children. But this, ladies and gentlemen, is the absolute worst hypocrisy of all. You see, Dan Barker is rabidly pro-abortion!

Articles on his FFRF.org website include "God Is Not So Pro-Life," and in another titled "What Does the Bible Say About Abortion" we read, "An embryo or fetus is not a human being." In an interview with Dinesh D'souza he said, "I support a woman's right to choose an abortion…I think for most women an abortion is a blessing in her life, it is a wonderful thing." (Ammi)

And he is pro-abortion in spite of the fact that he admits that position, according to his atheistic belief, takes all there is from a child. He said, "Since this is the only life we atheists have, each decision is crucial, and we are accountable for our actions right now... life is dear, it is fleeting, it is vibrant and vulnerable. It is heartbreaking. It can be lost. It will be lost. But we exist now. We are caring, intelligent animals, and we can treasure our brief lives." (Barker, "For Goodness Sake)

So, he pretends to be upset with God over the killing of children and fetuses in the womb, yet he himself has been an advocate of that which has led to the wholesale slaughter of more than fifty million babes in the womb. And according to his belief, this life was the only life those children would ever have, they did not go to heaven, they were just killed and put out of existence, and he is okay with that.

But he is not the only one. In fact, many of his fellow critics are even worse. Consider one of the leading "ethicists" in the world, Peter Singer, Professor of Bioethics at the Princeton University Center for Human Values. He is another one that hates the God he does not claim to believe in and views that non-existent God as unjust for ever taking human life. But just listen to what he believes:

"We can no longer base ethics on the idea that human beings are a special form of creation, made in the image of God, singled out from all other animals, and alone possessing an immortal soul...

"Once the religious mumbo-jumbo surrounding the term 'human' has been stripped away, we may continue to see normal members of our species as possessing greater capacities of rationality, self-consciousness, communication...than other members of any other species; but we will not regard as sacrosanct the life of each and every member of our species, no matter how limited its capacity for intelligent or even conscious life may be. If we compare a severely defective human infant with a ... dog or pig ... we will often find the nonhuman to have superior capacities... Species membership alone ... is not relevant... Humans who bestow superior value on the lives of all human beings, solely because they are members of our own species, are ... similar to... white racists..." (nrlc.org)

In a column titled "A Professor of Infanticide at Princeton," (Jewish World Review, 9/13/99) Nat Hentoff quotes from Singer's book *Practical Ethics*, (co-authored by Dr. Helga Kuhse):

> "Human babies are not born self-aware or capable of grasping that they exist over time. They are not persons." With animals being self-aware "the life of a newborn is of less value than the life of a pig, a dog, or a chimpanzee." And "a period of twenty-eight days after birth might be allowed before an infant is accepted as having the same right to live as others."

If you are still uncertain about what kind of ethicist Singer is, consider Michael Specter's article "The Dangerous Philosopher" in the *New Yorker* (9/6/99). Specter had lengthy conversations with Singer in Australia. He writes:

> "Singer believes, for example, that a human's life is not necessarily more sacred than a dog's, and that it might be more compassionate to carry out medical experiments on hopelessly disabled, unconscious orphans than on perfectly healthy rats."

> And "for Singer, killing is wrong because when you kill someone who wants to live you make it impossible for that person to fulfill his preferences. Obviously, if you kill somebody whose preferences don't have much chance of success-a severely disabled infant, for example, or somebody in an advanced stage of Alzheimer's disease-the moral equation becomes entirely different." Or

"killing a disabled infant is not morally equivalent to killing a person. Very often it is not wrong at all."

"When the death of a disabled infant will lead to the birth of another infant with better prospects of a happy life, the total amount of happiness will be greater if the disabled infant is killed. The loss of happy life for the first infant is outweighed by the gain of a happier life for the second. Therefore, if killing the hemophiliac infant has no adverse effect on others, it would, according to the total view, be right to kill him.

"That a fetus is known to be disabled is widely accepted as a grounds for abortion. Yet in discussing abortion, we say that birth does not mark a morally significant dividing line. I cannot see how one can defend the view that fetuses may be 'replaced' before birth, but newborn infants may not.

"If disabled newborn infants were not regarded as having a right to life until, say, a week or a month after birth it would allow parents, in consultation with their doctors, to choose on the basis of far greater knowledge of the infant's condition than is possible before birth." (46)

Singer, one of the most vocal modern skeptics of the Bible, a man who believes God is unjust any time He is involved in taking someone's life, believes that some humans are no better than animals, maybe even worse, babies should be able to be killed up to four weeks after they have been born for any reason at all or for no reason at all other than the whim of the parents, disabled people should be able to be experimented on like lab rats, and old people should be able to be killed when they are past the point of being useful.

Remind me again how unjust the God of the Old Testament was?

Here is another critic of the Bible, especially the God of the Old Testament:

> "An infant with severe brain damage, even if it survives for many years, may never learn to speak, and its mental powers may never rise above a primitive level. In fact, its psychological capacities may be markedly inferior to those of a typical Rhesus monkey. In that case, moral individualism would see no reason to prefer its life over that of the monkey's

> "Some unfortunate humans, perhaps because they have suffered brain damage, are not rational agents. What are we to say about them? The natural conclusion, according to the doctrine we are considering, would be that their status is that of mere animals. And perhaps we should go on to conclude that they may be used as nonhuman animals are used - perhaps as laboratory subjects, or as food." (James Rachels, 186)

James Rachels believed that God is unjust... and that human beings ought to be allowed to be used as food or as laboratory subjects, and that in many cases we ought to be more interested in keeping monkeys alive rather than humans.

Here is another shocking claim: "Many of us consider human fetuses in the first trimester to be more or less like rabbits, having imputed to them a range of happiness and suffering that does not grant them full status in our moral community." (Harris, 177)

Do you see the incredible hypocrisy? And this will be true of pretty much everyone you ever meet who wants to say nasty things about the God of the Old Testament. I have never, ever met a single one of them that was not pro-abortion. So, for your own benefit, an easy way to deal with anyone who tries to pick a fight with you on this subject is just to sweetly ask them, "Since you are so concerned with human life, let me ask you, are you in favor of abortion? Are you in favor of the killing of over fifty million babies since 1973? I'm just wondering because that is way, way, way more people than the God of the Old Testament ever put to death.

"Oh, and by the way, you say I shouldn't believe my Bible because God is a killer, so does that also mean I should not believe the writings of modern atheists and agnostics who advocate killing perfectly healthy babies up to twenty-eight days after they are born, and advocate doing lab experiments on disabled people, and advocate killing old people when they are no longer useful, and advocate infanticide as a means of population control?

"Oh, and by the way, are you okay with ripping a baby apart, limb by limb, literally ripping its legs and arms and heads off? Because that is what happens in an abortion. Are you okay with partial birth abortion, where a live baby is partially delivered, and then has scissors rammed into the back of its head and has its brain sucked out? Are you okay with that? Because if you think that all of that ought to be legal and protected, then it isn't God who is the monster, it is you who is the monster."

An examination of the Scriptures

Does God ever cause or command the death of people, especially in the Old Testament? Yes. And be honest, when you read it, does it not make you a bit uncomfortable? If it does, take comfort in this fact; it is supposed to.

God has built into each of us a respect for human life, because of how special it is:

Genesis 1:26 *And God said, Let us make man in our image, after our likeness: and let them have dominion over the fish of the sea, and over the fowl of the air, and over the* *cattle, and over all the earth, and over every creeping thing that creepeth upon the earth. 27 So God created man in his own image, in the image of God created he him; male and female created he them.*

Contrary to what people like Peter Singer believe, human life is more special and more valuable than any animal life. We alone are made in the image of God. Because of that, any time there is a human death it should bother us, even when that death is warranted and necessary. When a person breaks into your house to try and kill your wife and children, and you have to kill him to keep that from happening, it will probably still bother you for this very reason.

So, when we come to the Old Testament and see God bringing about death, especially when it seems like He is bringing about the death of innocents, it is going to bother us, and there is nothing wrong with that.

That being said, much of what is claimed about the "murderous God of the Old Testament" is completely untrue. Here are a few claims that I have been confronted with at various times:

"God teaches the use of a bizarre ritual using cursed "bitter water" to abort a fetus who was conceived through infidelity. (Numbers 5:11-21)"

No, He does not. That passage does not mention one thing about a woman being pregnant or losing a child. All it mentions is a way to prove whether or not she has been unfaithful.

"God caused rape and baby killing."

"Anyone who is captured will be run through with a sword. Their little children will be dashed to death right before their eyes. Their homes will be sacked, and their wives raped by the attacking hordes. For I will stir up the Medes against Babylon, and no amount of silver or gold will buy them off. The attacking armies will shoot down the young people with arrows. They will have no mercy on helpless babies and will show no compassion for the children. (Isaiah 13:15-18)"

No, God did not do any of this; Media did this. It was brought about by their own cruel treatment of others.

"God promised to destroy the infants of Samaria and rip open the stomachs of pregnant women."

"The people of Samaria must bear their guilt because they have rebelled against their God. They will fall by the sword; their little ones will be dashed to the ground, their pregnant women ripped open. (Hosea 13:16)"

God did not do this. He said that it would happen, but He did not command anyone to do it. The Assyrians came in and did it themselves, and the Assyrians did not follow Jehovah God, they did not even believe in Him.

So much of what you will see in the Old Testament is just exactly like this. People choose a course of action, and God says to them, "If you do this, I am going to remove my protective hand from you and let the enemy do whatever they want." Yet, despite the warning, people make their own choice. God gives them the free will to do so and then they experience the horrible consequences.

But there are some times in the Old Testament where God Himself directly commands killing or causes death.

In Numbers 16, Korah, Dathan, and Abiram rebelled against Moses and Aaron. Around three hundred people in the rebellion ended up being swallowed down into hell as the earth opened up to let them fall in. Is this an example of God being an unjust murderer? The God-hater will quickly say yes. But consider, there were two million people out in the wilderness needing to be cared for, and the only one God had enabled to do it was Moses. If this rebellion had not been dealt with quickly and harshly, the potential was there for many more to lose their lives, somewhere around two million in fact.

Did a man die in Numbers 15 for picking up sticks? Yes, we covered that in the second chapter of this book and found that he did what he did while in the presence of the Shekinah glory cloud of God, in the sight of all two million people, as a direct challenge to God. Once again, if it had not been dealt with quickly and harshly, the potential was there for many more to lose their lives.

Did Achan and his family get stoned to death in Joshua 7? Yes, but not until after their sin had caused the death of thirty-six innocent people.

Here is one to look at in some depth:

Numbers 31:1 *And the LORD spake unto Moses, saying,* **2** *Avenge the children of Israel of the Midianites: afterward shalt thou be gathered unto thy people.* **3** *And Moses spake unto the people, saying, Arm some of yourselves unto the war, and let them go against the Midianites, and avenge the LORD of Midian.* **4** *Of every tribe a thousand, throughout all the tribes of Israel, shall ye send to the war.* **5** *So there were delivered out of the thousands of Israel, a thousand of every tribe, twelve thousand armed for war.* **6** *And Moses sent them to the war, a thousand of every tribe, them and Phinehas the son of Eleazar the priest, to the war, with the holy instruments, and the trumpets to blow in his hand.* **7** *And they warred against the Midianites, as the LORD commanded Moses; and they slew all the males.* **8** *And they slew the kings of Midian, beside the rest of them that were slain; namely, Evi, and Rekem, and Zur, and Hur, and Reba, five kings of Midian: Balaam also the son of Beor they slew with the sword.* **9** *And the children of Israel took all the women of Midian captives, and their little ones, and took the spoil of all their cattle, and all their flocks, and all their goods.* **10** *And they burnt all their cities wherein they dwelt, and all their goodly castles, with fire.* **11** *And they took all the spoil, and all the prey, both of men and of beasts.* **12** *And they brought the captives, and the prey, and the spoil, unto Moses, and Eleazar the priest, and unto the congregation of the children of Israel, unto the camp at the plains of Moab, which are by Jordan near Jericho.* **13** *And Moses, and Eleazar the* *priest, and all the princes of the congregation, went forth to meet them without the camp. 14 And Moses was wroth with the officers of the host, with the captains over thousands, and captains over hundreds, which came from the battle. 15 And Moses said unto them, Have ye saved all the women alive? 16 Behold, these caused the children of Israel, through the counsel of Balaam, to commit trespass against the LORD in the matter of Peor, and there was a plague among the congregation of the LORD. 17 Now therefore kill every male among the little ones, and kill every woman that hath known man by lying with him.*

When we get to phrases like "kill every male among the little ones," my heart just drops. It hurts me to even read it. I am not going to pretend to be so super-spiritual that I actually like it. And do you know why? Because even God did not like it. It was necessary, but that does not mean it is pleasant or something to rejoice over. When an officer shoots someone, it is necessary, but they do not rejoice over it.

This was done for two reasons. We find the word "avenge" in verse two. In other words, there was something the Midianites had already done to Israel that caused this response. It goes all the way back to Numbers 22 where Moab and Midian teamed up to try to destroy Israel. Their first plan of attack did not work, but by chapter twenty-five, they found one that did. They got Israelite men hooked up with loose Midianite women. What Midian could not do by the sword, they got God to do for them by judgment. And that was their entire goal, to destroy Israel by any means possible.

When God told His people in Numbers 31 to destroy Midian because of it, it was judgment for what Midian had done. But it was also with an eye to the future. Every other nation was watching. Any softness in dealing with this would invite the same kinds of attacks over and over again.

But further than that, we need to understand just how young those children could be when taught to hate Jews forever. Just this week (the week of February 24, 2015) the news carried stories and showed videos of four and five-year-old children being trained by ISIS to hate and kill Jews and Christians. They were dressed like little soldiers, marching, receiving weapons training. At four and five years old!

A few years ago, I watched a news video even more frightening, where eighteen-month-old children were being taught to chant hateful things against Jews and Christians. This is not a new thing, and it is something that was clearly possible in each and every case where God gave a command like this.

Does that mean that God liked it or that we have to like it? No. God never rejoiced in the death of a little one. Men did:

Psalm 137:8 *O daughter of Babylon, who art to be destroyed; happy shall he be, that rewardeth thee as thou hast served us.* **9** *Happy shall he be, that taketh and dasheth thy little ones against the stones.*

This is another verse that the critics use to attempt to prove that God is a killer of children and that He likes it. But pay attention, and you will see something very different. It was neither God nor Israel who finally killed the little ones of Babylon. It was the Medes and the Persians who did that. And yes, they were happy about it! This verse was a prophecy of what was going to happen, not of something that God did Himself, and not something that He had His people to do in this case.

There is a time other than Numbers 31 that shows us God commanding the killing of children:

Deuteronomy 25:17 *Remember what Amalek did unto thee by the way, when ye were come forth out of Egypt;* **18** *How he met thee by the way, and smote the hindmost of thee, even all that were feeble behind thee, when thou wast faint and weary; and he feared not God.* **19** *Therefore it shall be, when the LORD thy God hath given thee rest from all thine enemies round about, in the land which the LORD thy God giveth thee for an inheritance to possess it, **that thou***

shalt blot out the remembrance of Amalek from under heaven; thou shalt not forget it.

That was God's command to kill every last Amalekite everywhere, no matter how young. The entire race was to be eradicated. That is the absolute harshest command of this sort that God ever gave. Here is where the Children of Israel were supposed to fulfill it and did not:

1 Samuel 15:1 *Samuel also said unto Saul, The LORD sent me to anoint thee to be king over his people, over Israel: now therefore hearken thou unto the voice of the words of the LORD.* **2** *Thus saith the LORD of hosts, I remember that which Amalek did to Israel, how he laid wait for him in the way, when he came up from Egypt.* **3** *Now go and smite Amalek, and utterly destroy all that they have, and spare them not; but* **slay both man and woman, infant and suckling,** *ox and sheep, camel and ass.*

Yes, that is babies verse three is referring to. And again, if that does not put a lump in your throat, something is wrong with you.

Look at how this played out:

1 Samuel 15:7 *And Saul smote the Amalekites from Havilah until thou comest to Shur, that is over against Egypt.* **8** *And he took Agag the king of the Amalekites alive, and utterly destroyed all the people with the edge of the sword.* **9** *But Saul and the people spared Agag, and the best of the sheep, and of the oxen, and of the fatlings, and the lambs, and all that was good, and would not utterly destroy them: but every thing that was vile and refuse, that they destroyed utterly.* **10** *Then came the word of the LORD unto Samuel, saying,* **11** *It repenteth me that I have set up Saul to be king: for he is turned back from following me, and hath not performed my commandments. And it grieved Samuel; and he cried unto the LORD all night.* **12** *And when Samuel rose early to meet Saul in the morning, it was told Samuel, saying, Saul came to Carmel, and, behold, he set him up a place, and is gone about, and passed on, and gone down to Gilgal.* **13**

And Samuel came to Saul: and Saul said unto him, Blessed be thou of the LORD: I have performed the commandment of the LORD. **14** *And Samuel said, What meaneth then this bleating of the sheep in mine ears, and the lowing of the oxen which I hear?* **15** *And Saul said, They have brought them from the Amalekites: for the people spared the best of the sheep and of the oxen, to sacrifice unto the LORD thy God; and the rest we have utterly destroyed.* **16** *Then Samuel said unto Saul, Stay, and I will tell thee what the LORD hath said to me this night. And he said unto him, Say on.* **17** *And Samuel said, When thou wast little in thine own sight, wast thou not made the head of the tribes of Israel, and the LORD anointed thee king over Israel?* **18** *And the LORD sent thee on a journey, and said, Go and utterly destroy the sinners the Amalekites, and fight against them until they be consumed.* **19** *Wherefore then didst thou not obey the voice of the LORD, but didst fly upon the spoil, and didst evil in the sight of the LORD?* **20** *And Saul said unto Samuel, Yea, I have obeyed the voice of the LORD, and have gone the way which the LORD sent me, and have brought Agag the king of Amalek, and have utterly destroyed the Amalekites.* **21** *But the people took of the spoil, sheep and oxen, the chief of the things which should have been utterly destroyed, to sacrifice unto the LORD thy God in Gilgal.* **22** *And Samuel said, Hath the LORD as great delight in burnt offerings and sacrifices, as in obeying the voice of the LORD? Behold, to obey is better than sacrifice, and to hearken than the fat of rams.* **23** *For rebellion is as the sin of witchcraft, and stubbornness is as iniquity and idolatry. Because thou hast rejected the word of the LORD, he hath also rejected thee from being king.* **24** *And Saul said unto Samuel, I have sinned: for I have transgressed the commandment of the LORD, and thy words: because I feared the people, and obeyed their voice.* **25** *Now therefore, I pray thee, pardon my sin, and turn again with me, that I may worship the LORD.* **26** *And Samuel said unto Saul, I will not return with thee: for thou hast rejected the word of the*

LORD, and the LORD hath rejected thee from being king over Israel. **27** *And as Samuel turned about to go away, he laid hold upon the skirt of his mantle, and it rent.* **28** *And Samuel said unto him, The LORD hath rent the kingdom of Israel from thee this day, and hath given it to a neighbour of thine, that is better than thou.* **29** *And also the Strength of Israel will not lie nor repent: for he is not a man, that he should repent.* **30** *Then he said, I have sinned: yet honour me now, I pray thee, before the elders of my people, and before Israel, and turn again with me, that I may worship the LORD thy God.* **31** *So Samuel turned again after Saul; and Saul worshipped the LORD.* **32** *Then said Samuel, Bring ye hither to me Agag the king of the Amalekites. And Agag came unto him delicately. And Agag said, Surely the bitterness of death is past.* **33** *And Samuel said, As thy sword hath made women childless, so shall thy mother be childless among women. And Samuel hewed Agag in pieces before the LORD in Gilgal.*

God commanded them to destroy all of Amalek. They disobeyed. They were also careless. They disobeyed by sparing Agag, but Samuel fixed that by killing Agag himself. But there is a verse in this chapter that you need to compare with another passage, or you will miss something very essential:

1 Samuel 15:8 *And he took Agag the king of the Amalekites alive, and utterly destroyed all the people with the edge of the sword.*

When it says he utterly destroyed all the people, multiple commentaries for a very specific reason have a note saying "all the people that came into their hands, all the people that they came across." Those commentaries are actually correct. They were looking for the king as a trophy, so they killed everyone else they found, but they saved him alive. But it turns out that they were careless and missed some people. More about that in a moment.

The reason given for destroying all of them was stated in the book of Deuteronomy.

104

Deuteronomy 25:17 *Remember what Amalek did unto thee by the way, when ye were come forth out of Egypt;* **18** *How he met thee by the way, and smote the hindmost of thee, even all that were feeble behind thee, when thou wast faint and weary; and he feared not God.* **19** *Therefore it shall be, when the LORD thy God hath given thee rest from all thine enemies round about, in the land which the LORD thy God giveth thee for an inheritance to possess it, that thou shalt blot out the remembrance of Amalek from under heaven; thou shalt not forget it.*

Like a pack of wolves, Amalek, without any provocation, attacked Israel. Not the army of Israel, the little ones, the slow ones, the sick ones, the ones that could not defend themselves. That did not sit well with God, and His judgment on them was to tell Israel to wipe them out.

Once again, we see that this was not started by God or Israel. Nonetheless, when we see God commanding to kill them all, even the children, we get such a lump in our throats! But do you know what we have not mentioned in any of this? The omniscience of God. The fact that God knows the future.

At least one little Amalakite escaped that day. Actually, a great many, most likely. Look at verse thirty-three:

1 Samuel 15:33 *And Samuel said, As thy sword hath made women childless, so shall thy mother be childless among women. And Samuel hewed Agag in pieces before the LORD in Gilgal.*

Samuel specifically mentioned Agag's mother. She was obviously not the only one in the nation left behind, either. And whoever had been left or spared went on to have kids and grandkids and great grandkids.

Fast forward several hundred years to the time when most of Israel was in Persia. There was a Jew there, Mordecai, who would not worship a man who wanted to be worshipped. That man's name was Haman. How did Haman respond to something as simple as Mordecai not worshiping him? He decided to kill every Jew in the entire world! And he almost succeeded. But here is what you might want to pay attention to:

Esther 3:1 *After these things did king Ahasuerus promote Haman the son of Hammedatha* **the Agagite***, and advanced him, and set his seat above all the princes that were with him.*

Not once, not twice, but five times in this book he is called "Haman the Agagite." He was descended from that same Agag, the Amalekite king in 1 Samuel 15. The children of Israel got careless, they did not kill everyone, and years later, it almost cost them in the form of a literal holocaust years before there ever was a Hitler.

Only God could have known that. The omniscience of God is very often the reason for why He does what He does, including things that make us uncomfortable.

"But wait! Those children still were innocent, even though they would have grown up to be evil, and even though their descendants were going to be mass murderers!"

Well, there may be one other thing you want to consider. According to the atheist's view, who do not mind the killing of children as long as it is them who do it instead of God, when those kids are dead, they are done. They have had everything taken from them.

But what is the real truth, the Bible truth? The real truth is that every one of them was and is an eternal soul who will spend eternity in heaven or hell. And based on their family's and nation's worship of false gods like Moloch, who, by the way, demanded infant sacrifice by burning certain children alive, those kids were going to grow up, grow old, die, and go to hell.

But the Bible teaches clearly that when an innocent child dies, it goes to heaven. If you could go to heaven today and speak to any of them, would they have any complaints with God at all? None. None at all.

This chapter has been very long, so let me give you some points to summarize it.

1.	Many of the popular critics who rail against "the God who kills" are the world's biggest hypocrites, because they and their kind have promoted more killing than God ever dreamed of, just by abortion alone.

2.	Many of the popular critics who rail against "the God who kills" are also the world's biggest hypocrites because they view life as so worthless that even a perfectly healthy baby can be killed, a month after it is born, just because the parents want to and because they believe it is acceptable to kill "defective" humans and old humans when they are "no longer useful." Their supposed horror at God taking life is a mask to cover up the monsters that they really are.

3.	Anyone who is pro-abortion is a hypocrite to rail against "the God who kills"

4.	People who do not believe in God have no right to accuse Him of doing wrong since they themselves admit that there is no absolute standard of right and wrong and that in their own view, absolutely everything can be justified given the right circumstances.

5.	The vast majority of times in the Old Testament that God did bring about death, it was because of the gravest of wickedness that had already been done or because of the worst of harm that was going to be done. God never, ever ended life capriciously or arbitrarily.

6.	Most of the cases the scoffers point to of "God killing children" are outright lies. When you actually take time to read the accounts, He merely prophesied what people like the Assyrians or Medes and Persians were going to do.

7.	In the exceedingly rare cases where God did bring about the death of children, those children went to heaven, and massive damage in the future was averted. Further, those children were often taught from infancy to hate and kill the Jews.

8.   Most importantly, death was never in God's original plan to begin with. It was mankind that knowingly allowed sin and death to enter into our world. If it had not been for that, not one person would have died, ever. We humans are responsible for all of the death that people love to blame God for.

9.   God Himself, the supposed killer, willingly died Himself so that He could one glorious day kill death itself. We who are saved will get to live forever and be with our saved loved ones forever, and death will not even be a memory.

Chapter Eight
A Problem Called Polygamy

If you ever bother to take your Bible and show a critic what it says about the subject of marriage, you will very likely at some point be confronted with an accusation that goes something like this:

"Well, why should I believe that? After all, the Bible, especially the Old Testament, allowed polygamy! And if the Bible allows polygamy, and you are now against it, why shouldn't I be against everything the Bible says? After all, it is clearly outdated."

So, what are we to make of that? Allow me to begin by asking and answering a question.

Can you find examples of polygamy in the Bible?

Yes, absolutely. Here are a few notable ones:

1 Kings 11:1 *But king Solomon loved many strange women, together with the daughter of Pharaoh, women of the Moabites, Ammonites, Edomites, Zidonians, and Hittites;* **2** *Of the nations concerning which the LORD said unto the children of Israel, Ye shall not go in to them, neither shall they come in unto you: for surely they will turn away your heart after their gods: Solomon clave unto these in love.* **3** *And he had seven hundred wives, princesses, and three hundred concubines: and his wives turned away his heart.* **4** *For it came to pass, when Solomon was old, that his wives* *turned away his heart after other gods: and his heart was not perfect with the LORD his God, as was the heart of David his father.*

1 Samuel 25:39 And when David heard that Nabal was dead, he said, Blessed be the LORD, that hath pleaded the cause of my reproach from the hand of Nabal, and hath kept his servant from evil: for the LORD hath returned the wickedness of Nabal upon his own head. And David sent and communed with Abigail, to take her to him to wife. 40 And when the servants of David were come to Abigail to Carmel, they spake unto her, saying, David sent us unto thee, to take thee to him to wife. 41 And she arose, and bowed herself on her face to the earth, and said, Behold, let thine handmaid be a servant to wash the feet of the servants of my lord. 42 And Abigail hasted, and arose, and rode upon an ass, with five damsels of hers that went after her; and she went after the messengers of David, and became his wife. 43 David also took Ahinoam of Jezreel; and they were also both of them his wives.

Genesis 29:18 And Jacob loved Rachel; and said, I will serve thee seven years for Rachel thy younger daughter. 19 And Laban said, It is better that I give her to thee, than that I should give her to another man: abide with me. 20 And Jacob served seven years for Rachel; and they seemed unto him but a few days, for the love he had to her. 21 And Jacob said unto Laban, Give me my wife, for my days are fulfilled, that I may go in unto her. 22 And Laban gathered together all the men of the place, and made a feast. 23 And it came to pass in the evening, that he took Leah his daughter, and brought her to him; and he went in unto her. 24 And Laban gave unto his daughter Leah Zilpah his maid for an handmaid. 25 And it came to pass, that in the morning, behold, it was Leah: and he said to Laban, What is this thou hast done unto me? did not I serve with thee for Rachel? wherefore then hast thou beguiled me? 26 And Laban said, It must not be so done in our country, to give the younger before the firstborn. **27** *Fulfil her week, and we will give thee this also for the service which thou shalt serve with me yet seven other years.* **28** *And Jacob did so, and fulfilled her week: and he gave him Rachel his daughter to wife also.*

Genesis 4:19 *And Lamech took unto him two wives: the name of the one was Adah, and the name of the other Zillah.*

Genesis 28:8 *And Esau seeing that the daughters of Canaan pleased not Isaac his father;* **9** *Then went Esau unto Ishmael, and took unto the wives which he had Mahalath the daughter of Ishmael Abraham's son, the sister of Nebajoth, to be his wife.*

2 Chronicles 11:21 *And Rehoboam loved Maachah the daughter of Absalom above all his wives and his concubines: (for he took eighteen wives, and threescore concubines; and begat twenty and eight sons, and threescore daughters.)*

Esau, Lamech, David, Jacob, Solomon, and Rehoboam were all polygamists. So yes, we can most certainly find examples of polygamy in the Old Testament. But the fact that you can find examples of something does not necessarily mean that it is either right or ideal. For instance, what else can you find just in the lives of those same six polygamists?

Esau: a heathen who despised his birthright, one who was so carnal that God said He hated him.

Lamech: a killer, and a man consumed with pride.

David: an adulterer, a liar, a murderer.

Jacob: a man who lied to his own old, blind father, a man whose name means trickster, a man who stole from his brother.

Solomon: not just a polygamist, but a SUPER polygamist, a man who was so soaked in worldly pleasure that he eventually decided that all of life was vanity, an idolater.

Rehoboam: a man who caused a civil war.

111

So, the fact that we see examples of anything does not necessarily mean that it was right or ideal. If it does, then not only is polygamy allowable and ideal, so are all of the other things those men did.

But when you are looking at the Old Testament and what it says about polygamy, what you really might want to take note of is how very few examples of it people can point to when compared to all of the normal, right, traditional monogamous marriages. There really are only a tiny handful of examples of polygamy, and multitudes upon multitudes of examples of monogamy.

So here is a second question:

Did God often allow polygamy and even give instructions concerning it?

Once again, the answer is yes. Here are some verses to look at:

Exodus 21:7 *And if a man sell his daughter to be a maidservant, she shall not go out as the menservants do.* **8** *If she please not her master, who hath betrothed her to himself, then shall he let her be redeemed: to sell her unto a strange nation he shall have no power, seeing he hath dealt deceitfully with her.* **9** *And if he have betrothed her unto his son, he shall deal with her after the manner of daughters.* **10** *If he take him another wife; her food, her raiment, and her duty of marriage, shall he not diminish.*

This was God instructing that if a man took a second wife, he still had to fully take care of the first. But pay very close attention to a matter of timing on this and on the next reference in the law to polygamy. The Children of Israel had been enslaved in a foreign, polygamous land for four hundred plus years (historyembalmed.org). The fact that God gave instructions in the law for how to treat multiple wives is not an indicator that polygamy was to be regarded as normal and right, it is an indicator of the present reality of people who had been taught wrong on the subject for four centuries.

Deuteronomy 21:15 *If a man have two wives, one beloved, and another hated, and they have born him children, both the beloved and the hated; and if the firstborn son be hers that was hated:* **16** *Then it shall be, when he maketh his sons to inherit that which he hath, that he may not make the son of the beloved firstborn before the son of the hated, which is indeed the firstborn:* **17** *But he shall acknowledge the son of the hated for the firstborn, by giving him a double portion of all that he hath: for he is the beginning of his strength; the right of the firstborn is his.*

This was God instructing that a man with more than one wife who hated one of them could not cheat the firstborn out of his birthright if he happened to be born by the one he hated.

There is one passage, though, that more than most others seems to indicate that polygamy is acceptable to God:

2 Samuel 12:7 *And Nathan said to David, Thou art the man. Thus saith the LORD God of Israel, I anointed thee king over Israel, and I delivered thee out of the hand of Saul;* **8** *And I gave thee thy master's house, and thy master's wives into thy bosom, and gave thee the house of Israel and of Judah; and if that had been too little, I would moreover have given unto thee such and such things.*

This was God reminding David that he had grievously sinned by taking Bathsheba. When He told him that, he reminded him of all the things He had given him, including his master, former king Saul's wives.

Very briefly, let us examine each of those sets of instructions. The first one, God instructing that if a man took a second wife, he still had to fully take care of the first, certainly was appreciated by any first wives out there. Polygamy was very, very common in the ancient world, mostly because there were vastly more women than men. This was because of the high early mortality rate of men since almost every man went to war. Women were not normally able to provide for themselves, so polygamy just became the normal thing to do, and wives of Israelite men enjoyed protections that wives of other men did not have, including this one.

Second, God instructing that a man with more than one wife who hated one of them could not cheat the firstborn out of his birthright if he happened to be born by the one he hated, was certainly appreciated by those sons.

The third one is the most interesting one, by far. When God said what He said to David, He let us in on an interesting custom of the ancient world. When a king defeated a rival king, everything that defeated king had went to the new king. Wives were at the top of that list since to have a king's wives was the greatest of insults to him. This was a punishment to Saul for his disobedience. But does it indicate that polygamy is right or ideal? No, none of them do.

If God allowing something or giving instructions on something means that it is right or ideal, then even slavery must be considered right and ideal, and from our chapter on slavery, you know that is not the view of Scripture.

Here is an extremely important verse that you need to keep in mind. It is from the New Testament, but it is about the Old Testament times:

Acts 17:29 *Forasmuch then as we are the offspring of God, we ought not to think that the Godhead is like unto gold, or silver, or stone, graven by art and man's device.* **30** *And the times of this ignorance God winked at; but now commandeth all men every where to repent:*

This was Paul on Mars Hill, dealing largely with the subject of idolatry. In so doing he referred back to older times as "the times of this ignorance," and said that God "winked at it," but now commands men everywhere to repent. In other words, people in the times of the Old Testament did not know all that we know, and because of that, God let them get by with some things that He did not necessarily approve of. That being the case, things that God let people get by with, even things that He gave instructions on, may not be right or ideal;

they may just be examples of God being patient with people who did not know better.

Polygamy is very clearly one of those things.

Yes, it happened in the Old Testament, but no, it is not ever the way it was supposed to be.

What does the Bible say that lets us know that polygamy was at best, less than ideal, and at worst, outright wrong?

To start answering that question, let us go back to the beginning.

Genesis 2:21 *And the LORD God caused a deep sleep to fall upon Adam, and he slept: and he took one of his ribs, and closed up the flesh instead thereof;* **22** *And the rib, which the LORD God had taken from man, made he a woman, and brought her unto the man.* **23** *And Adam said, This is now bone of my bones, and flesh of my flesh: she shall be called Woman, because she was taken out of Man.* **24** *Therefore shall a man leave his father and his mother, and shall cleave unto his wife: and they shall be one flesh.* **25** *And they were both naked, the man and his wife, and were not ashamed.*

Notice that God made just one man and one woman and that in verse twenty-four He applied that one-and-one-only formula to all succeeding generations. Jesus Himself later made an authoritative statement exactly like that, one that gives us the very foundation for monogamy:

Matthew 19:1 *And it came to pass, that when Jesus had finished these sayings, he departed from Galilee, and came into the coasts of Judaea beyond Jordan;* **2** *And great multitudes followed him; and he healed them there.* **3** *The Pharisees also came unto him, tempting him, and saying unto him, Is it lawful for a man to put away his wife for every cause?* **4** *And he answered and said unto them,* ***Have ye not read, that he which made them at the beginning made them male and female****,* **5** *And said, For this cause shall a man*

115

leave father and mother, and shall cleave to his wife: and they twain shall be one flesh? **6** *Wherefore they are no more twain, but one flesh. What therefore God hath joined together, let not man put asunder.* **7** *They say unto him, Why did Moses then command to give a writing of divorcement, and to put her away?* **8** *He saith unto them, Moses because of the hardness of your hearts suffered you to put away your wives:* **but from the beginning it was not so.**

In the context of marriage, twice Jesus went right back to the very beginning. He established that when it comes to marriage, the standard we go by is the very first one: one man plus one woman, period, never to be put asunder.

Is there any significance to this? Yes, oh yes:

Ephesians 5:25 *Husbands, love your wives, even as Christ also loved the church, and gave himself for it;* **26** *That he might sanctify and cleanse it with the washing of water by the word,* **27** *That he might present it to himself a glorious church, not having spot, or wrinkle, or any such thing; but that it should be holy and without blemish.* **28** *So ought men to love their wives as their own bodies. He that loveth his wife loveth himself.* **29** *For no man ever yet hated his own flesh; but nourisheth and cherisheth it, even as the Lord the church:* **30** *For we are members of his body, of his flesh, and of his bones.* **31** *For this cause shall a man leave his father and mother, and shall be joined unto his wife, and they two shall be one flesh.* **32** *This is a great mystery: but I speak concerning Christ and the church.*

The Lord Jesus Christ has exactly one love, exactly one bride, the saved, the church. The marriage of one man and one woman was designed to mirror that. Marriage is a picture of Christ and the church. No wonder the church has normally taken a stand against polygamy; they knew the Bible well enough to know what marriage represents.

Is there anything to fear about the Old Testament? No, not even a few isolated episodes of polygamy. God may have in mercy and patience winked at different things on which mankind was ignorant, but that does not change His original intent one bit: one man, one woman, for life.

Chapter Nine
A Job to Get Past Job

I was unaware until a recent kerfuffle with angry atheists that they take great umbrage with the book of Job. When they made me aware of that, I started doing some homework and, sure enough, a great many scoffers and critics of the Old Testament love to focus in on the book of Job to try and destroy people's faith not just in the Old Testament but in the character of God. Let me give you a sample I found from a very angry person who did not divulge his or her name. If anyone can find out who he or she is and source this information, I will be glad to give them the credit they deserve for their "work." You will notice I have to use _____ a lot, because the "tolerance above all else" crowd is, as usual, blasphemously intolerant.

"On May 9th, Billy Graham received a letter from a woman in despair. She is undergoing chemotherapy, and she e-mailed him to ask if she was being punished for something that she had done in her life. Graham's response is that God isn't necessarily inflicting consequences on her life, but might be allowing them to happen without intervening for a variety of reasons.

"Though I agree with Graham on the point that cancer or physical illness isn't a consequence rained down from heaven, that might be the extent of our agreement. This woman, suffering from cancer, should never view it as a consequence unless she has made a habit of smoking, eating an unhealthy diet, or excessive drinking and/or drug use. And I wouldn't say that cancer is ever deserved, so please don't misunderstand my comments here. The fact remains, that even if God allows bad things to happen instead of directly causing them, he's still an _____.

"If you are familiar with the story of Job, then you'll know that the essence of it is that Job was extraordinarily wealthy. He owned land, lots of livestock, and had a beautiful wife. He praised and thanked God every day. But one day, God approached Satan and began gloating about Job's undeniable faith. Satan encouraged God to stop providing blessings and wealth and bet God that if Job lost all of his possessions, wealth, and family, that he would curse God. So, God, being the giant _____ that he is, put it to the test! Job began suffering boils on his face, and then wind blew which caused his home to collapse and kill his sons and daughters. His servants and livestock were slaughtered. He lost everything. And his wife and friends told him to curse God. But he got down on his hands and knees and said, 'The Lord giveth and the Lord taketh away, blessed is the name of the Lord.' Satan lost his bet.

"Christians frequently refer to the story of Job when the chips are down. They retell how Job stayed strong in his faith, and encourage each other to remain strong in their faiths, too. It's nice that they can look at the positives, but let's take a closer look at the kind of character that God must have.

"In Job 1:8, God directly gloats to Satan about his servant Job. Like that _____ in high school whose parents bought him a new car, and he parks it conspicuously in the student parking lot and makes _____ sure that everyone can see it. This is the Judeo-Christian God.

"In Job chapter 1 verse 16:

"'While he was yet speaking, there came also another, and said, The fire of God is fallen from heaven, and hath burned up the sheep, and the servants, and consumed them; and I only am escaped alone to tell thee.'

"Many Christians justify that God allowed these bad things to happen to Job, and did not perpetrate them. But, it is apparent here that God is responsible for at least some of these atrocities. Again, even if he just allows these things to happen without any intervention, that's a significant testament to God's _____ character.

"What kind of _____ kills your kids, servants, livestock, and blows your house down just to see if you still love him, anyway? I have a loving relationship with my girlfriend. I don't feel the need to destroy her things or send her through a period of tribulation to make sure that she loves me for me and not the fact that we have a nice TV and good food in the fridge.

"This gives me a great opportunity to point out a hideous contradiction in the Bible: Bible-thumping Christians consistently speak of God knowing the hearts of 'his children', and how he can spot an unbeliever. This God is all-knowing, but yet he can't determine whether or not Job is genuine in his character?

"Answer: [Cue illogical and irrational Christian apologetic that I don't care about]

"In Job 9:17, 22-24:

"17: For he breaketh me with a tempest, and multiplieth my wounds without cause;

"22-24: This is one thing, therefore I said it, He destroyeth the perfect and the wicked. If the scourge slay suddenly, he will laugh at the trial of the innocent. The earth is given into the hand of the wicked: he covereth the faces of the judges thereof; if not, where, and who is he?'

"God seems to have this _____ inclination toward evil and violence. He'll destroy not only the wicked, but he'll take down the perfect, too? I guess it's good that nobody is perfect! He'll laugh at the trial of the innocent? So God is going to LAUGH at injustice, even though he hates that? And Christians want God's justice to be the model of our judicial systems? Please!

"Perhaps one of the most offensive parts of this story is that God smote the lives of Job's servants, children, and livestock just to prove a point. What an _____!

"Job isn't even the best reference to God's propensity toward atrocious, genocidal, hateful, and _____ like behavior. But in the very specific case of Job, God absolutely obliterates Job because Satan told him that if he did, Job wouldn't remain

122

faithful. That makes God a _____
and Job an idiot. Have at it."

I have done some checking. This anonymous critic's opinion is not an isolated one. Most every rabid critic you will ever meet holds the exact same opinion and uses this Old Testament book as a battering ram. Clearly, they have quite a job to get past Job! But are these people right, in anything? It is my contention that the book of Job, far from undermining our faith in God, ought to actually strengthen it! So let us dissect the complaints. In fact, let us utterly obliterate them and then go from there to tell you the things about the book of Job that they fear to get anywhere near.

Let us begin by dealing with the character of the complainer, specifically the fact that while accusing God of poor character, he himself is a liar. Look at this early quote once again, and see what you notice:

"If you are familiar with the story of Job, then you'll know that the essence of it is that Job was extraordinarily wealthy. He owned land, lots of livestock, and had a beautiful wife. He praised and thanked God every day. But one day, God approached Satan and began gloating about Job's undeniable faith."

Do you see the lie? Who approached whom! Read it and see:

Job 1:1 *There was a man in the land of Uz, whose name was Job; and that man was perfect and upright, and one that feared God, and eschewed evil.* **2** *And there were born unto him seven sons and three daughters.* **3** *His substance also was seven thousand sheep, and three thousand camels, and five hundred yoke of oxen, and five hundred she asses, and a very great household; so that this man was the greatest of all the men of the east.* **4** *And his sons went and feasted in their houses, every one his day; and sent and called for their three sisters to eat and to drink with them.* **5** *And it was so, when the days of their feasting were gone about, that Job sent and sanctified them, and rose up early in the* *morning, and offered burnt offerings according to the number of them all: for Job said, It may be that my sons have sinned, and cursed God in their hearts. Thus did Job continually.* **6** *Now there was a day when the sons of God came to present themselves before the LORD, and Satan came also among them.* **7** *And the LORD said unto Satan, Whence comest thou? Then Satan answered the LORD, and said, From going to and fro in the earth, and from walking up and down in it.* **8** *And the LORD said unto Satan, Hast thou considered my servant Job, that there is none like him in the earth, a perfect and an upright man, one that feareth God, and escheweth evil?*

The critic paints a picture of Satan minding his own sweet, peaceful business, and God going looking for him so that he can brag about Job. But the very opposite is true. Satan, as always, was roaming the earth looking for good people to attack. But a very merciful God kept him on a leash, and the very devil himself was forced to come before God and give a report of his comings and goings. So, it was not God approaching Satan, it was Satan approaching God. And it was not God pointing out to Satan some guy he had never noticed, he was pointing out to Satan the very man that He knew Satan had noticed above all else. Satan was able to instantly recount for God every detail of Job's life! This critic and others know this, they just do not care. It is much more fun for them to lie about God than it is to tell the truth about Him.

Let us notice something else. And you will find this to be very, very consistent among these people. Who is it that did all of the damage to Job? Satan:

Job 1:12 *And the LORD said unto Satan, Behold, **all that he hath is in thy power**; only upon himself put not forth **thine hand**. So Satan went forth from the presence of the LORD.*

Job 2:6 *And the LORD said unto Satan, Behold, **he is in thine hand**; but save his life.* *7 So went **Satan forth from***

the presence of the LORD, and smote Job with sore boils *from the sole of his foot unto his crown.*

God never put a finger on Job. Every bit of pain he experienced was at the hands of the devil. But please notice this: how many times does the author of this hit piece on God say a negative word about the devil? None. How many times does he curse the devil? None. Do you get any sense at all that he hates the devil? No. In fact, listen to a word he uses of the devil:

"Satan **encouraged** God to stop providing blessings and wealth."

Would it have ever crossed your mind to use such a positive word as "encouraged" to describe the devil and what he does? This is intentional! He uses the word "encouraged" in reference to the devil. He never utters an unkind word about the devil, but he curses God ten times in words so vile I cannot repeat them in any company! It is very clear that this man literally hates God, which is the height of irony since he claims to believe that God does not exist! How do you literally hate someone that does not exist?

When people are very careful to avoid saying anything bad about Satan, yet blaspheme God every other breath, it is not that they do not believe in God; it is that they have chosen the other side and are fighting against God.

Let us continue.

"This woman, suffering from cancer, should never view it as a consequence unless she has made a habit of smoking, eating an unhealthy diet, or excessive drinking and/or drug use."

I am giving you this quote once again because of how clearly it demonstrates the inconsistency and outright hypocrisy of the scoffers. Please notice the words "unhealthy" and "excessive" and the negative reference to drug use. May I ask, are those things not judging? Who gets to decide what is excessive? How dare you question anyone's

125

drug use! How dare you refer to something as "unhealthy!" You see, you will find that the very crowd that despises the "thou shalts and thou shalt nots" of Scripture are themselves the most judgmental individuals anywhere.

If you eat meat, you are a murderer of innocent animals. If you live in a big house or drive an SUV, you are raping the environment. If you vote conservative, you are (exact quote here from the comments on a news story about Christians) "a Neanderthal who should immediately go drink cyanide." You will never find more judgmental, hateful people on earth than people like this guy who accuse God of being mean and judgmental!

Let us keep going.

"The fact remains, that even if God allows bad things to happen instead of directly causing them, he's still an _____."

The argument this man is using is basically this: unless God stops evil from happening, He Himself is evil. Whenever you are confronted with that argument, here is what your response should be: "Okay, what if He decided to start with your evil deeds, would that be okay?"

Suddenly you will hear the tune beginning to change...

"Uh, wait, that's not what I meant!"

Yes, I know that is not what you meant. You see, you, sir, want to still have all of your free will. You want to be allowed to fornicate and drink and do drugs. You want to be allowed to curse and blaspheme. You want to be allowed to offend whomever you choose. You even want the right to kill people if your particular world-view calls for it, such as this pesky little thing called abortion which has slaughtered more than fifty million babies. You want to have all of your free will, and you would be violently angry if God took it from you; you just do not want anyone *else* to have a free will! Since God did not miraculously stop the Holocaust by killing all of the Nazis, He must be evil, and you have a huge problem with Him. But if God did miraculously stop abortion by killing all of the doctors who do it, you would still regard Him as evil and have a huge problem with Him!

Muslims in many places around the world hate Israel and America and are killing people in droves. But if God suddenly took their free will and turned them into Israel loving, American flag waving, "Amazing Grace" singing robots, you, sir, would be bitterly angry with God for doing that, since you despise the Jews and do not really too much like America or "Amazing Grace."

But you see, if anyone is allowed to have a free will, then it would be unequal not to allow everyone to have a free will. And if people or angels or devils have a free will, then bad things are going to happen, and God is normally going to allow it, no matter how brutal. Should we still pray? Certainly. Does God sometimes respond to those prayers in miraculous ways? Yes. Should we expect that to be the norm? No. If it was, then free will is gone, and God will not take the free will of man from Him.

Think of it this way. The most precious thing we have is also the most dangerous thing we have. Nothing allows for greater good or greater evil than this thing called free will. I would not trade it for anything, and yet it is that very thing that allows for all of the evils and atrocities on earth. I used my free will to accept Christ. I use my free will to serve God and to do kind things for others. A young mother recently used her free will to refuse cancer treatments while pregnant. She willingly gave up her life so her baby could live. But others use their free will for murder and destruction. God does not force me to do right, and He does not force others to not do wrong.

Never blame God for evil simply because He allows it, and never allow anyone else to do so either because the only other alternative would be the complete removal of our free will.

Let us keep going.

127

"What kind of -------------- kills your kids, servants, livestock, and blows your house down just to see if you still love him, anyway? I have a loving relationship with my girlfriend. I don't feel the need to destroy her things or send her through a period of tribulation to make sure that she loves me for me and not the fact that we have a nice TV and good food in the fridge.

"This gives me a great opportunity to point out a hideous contradiction in the Bible: Bible-thumping Christians consistently speak of God knowing the hearts of 'his children', and how he can spot an unbeliever. This God is all-knowing, but yet he can't determine whether or not Job is genuine in his character?"

Once again it is necessary to point out that this man is intentionally dishonest with Scripture: God is not the one who did any of this. Secondly, his entire premise is both assumed and incorrect. None of this was done so that God could "see if Job still loved Him." None of it was done because God was "trying to determine whether or not Job was genuine in his character." The book of Job does not say or teach that from God's mouth anywhere. And even when God does ask a question in the Bible, it is not for His benefit, but for ours. This man reduces the trial of Job to nothing more than a kindergarten letter with an "I love you do you love me, check yes or no" box. Nothing in the book of Job supports that view.

What Job went through was not for God's benefit, it was not even entirely for Job's benefit. Do you know who the greatest beneficiaries of Job's trials have been? Us! Four thousand years of believers have benefitted from what he went through. Eternal truths come out of this book that have helped countless millions. Job wanted to get out of the trial then, but I guarantee you that now, looking down from heaven, seeing the good that has come from it, he would not change a thing.

Let us continue.

"In Job 9:17, 22-24:

"17: For he breaketh me with a tempest, and multiplieth my wounds without cause;

"22-24: This is one thing, therefore I said it, He destroyeth the perfect and the wicked. If the scourge slay suddenly, he will laugh at the trial of the innocent. The earth is given into the hand of the wicked: he covereth the faces of the judges thereof; if not, where, and who is he?'

"God seems to have this _____ inclination toward evil and violence. He'll destroy not only the wicked, but he'll take down the perfect, too? I guess it's good that nobody is perfect! He'll laugh at the trial of the innocent? So, God is going to LAUGH at injustice, even though he hates that? And Christians want God's justice to be the model of our judicial systems? Please!"

I have a very difficult time finding something nice to say about this because literally, the only two options I find here are either dishonesty or ignorance. This critic uses the words of Job as if they were accurate and true. He seems unaware of or dishonest about the fact that even in the Bible, people said things that were not correct, and that God accurately recorded it.

Have you, either in the heat of the moment or in the midst of a devastating trial, said something that you later regretted? Did you then hope that people who heard it would cut you some slack?

In the midst of his worst moment, Job said some things about God that were not true. But he also managed to say some things that were true. Just like us, Job was capable of getting it right one moment and wrong at another.

Now here is the interesting thing; this scoffer takes the words of Job as true when he speaks ill of God, but conveniently ignores other things that Job said about God, such as these:

Job 19:25 *For I know that my redeemer liveth, and that he shall stand at the latter day upon the earth:* **26** *And though after my skin worms destroy this body, yet in my flesh shall I see God:*

Job 42:1 *Then Job answered the LORD, and said,* **2** *I know that thou canst do every thing, and that no thought can be withholden from thee.* **3** *Who is he that hideth counsel without knowledge? therefore have I uttered that I understood not; things too wonderful for me, which I knew not.*

Pardon me, Mr. Blasphemer, do you believe what Job said about God being a destroyer of the perfect?

"Yes! Yes, I do!"

Well pardon me, Mr. Blasphemer, do you believe what Job said about God being real and alive and that one day we will stand before Him? Do you believe what Job said about having spoken ill of God without really having complete knowledge?

"Uhhhhhhh..."

Here is the amazing thing, and please let this sink in, this scoffer and others like him read the book of Job and use it as an excuse to not believe in God. But the Job who literally lived through it all did believe in Him. He believed in Him before the trial, during the trial, and after the trial. So, who exactly is it who looks very foolish when you examine their view of the book of Job?

Here is his last quote:

"Perhaps one of the most offensive
parts of this story is that God smote the lives

of Job's servants, children, and livestock just to   prove   a   point.   What   an
_____!

     "Job isn't even the best reference to God's propensity toward atrocious, genocidal, hateful, and _____ like behavior. But in the very specific case of Job, God absolutely obliterates Job because Satan told him that if he did, Job wouldn't remain faithful.   That   makes   God   a _____ and Job an idiot. Have at it."

No sir, God did not do any of that. Satan did that, the one character in the entire story that you for some reason decide to speak well of. God you blaspheme; Job, whom you initially feign sympathy for, you call an idiot.

So what do we conclude? Just like critics everywhere, the devil gets a complete pass, since they actually like him, but the God they claim does not exist, and everyone who believes in Him, they curse and blaspheme.

In short, their very hatred and dishonesty serve as a spotlight on the fact that they do actually believe in both God and the Bible, including the Old Testament, they just hate Him and it. Let me show you the passage of Scripture that best describes them:

Psalm 2:1 *Why do the heathen rage, and the people imagine a vain thing?* **2** *The kings of the earth set themselves, and the rulers take counsel together, against the LORD, and against his anointed, saying,* **3** *Let us break their bands asunder, and cast away their cords from us.*

You see, it is not that people are ambivalent and unconcerned about the God who does not exist and about the Bible which is not true. It is that they know He is real, they know the Word is true, they have just made up their minds to join Team Satan and rebel against God and His Word.

But let us change course just for a bit. You see, in using the book of Job as a battering ram, they have opened the door for things that they dearly hope you will never notice. But you will notice them because I am going to show you. You see, there are things in the book of Job that so clearly show the Bible to be the Word of God that any honest person would have to admit it. Let us have a look.

Job 26:7 *He stretcheth out the north over the empty place, and hangeth the earth upon nothing.*

The book of Job is one of the oldest written documents on earth, dating most likely to around 2500 B.C. It is some four thousand or more years old. Can anyone tell me what "science" was like four thousand years ago?

Let me ask it this way. Way back then, what did people commonly believe about the earth? Take your pick. Some believed that it was riding through space on the back of a turtle. Some believed it was held up on a giant's shoulders. There are many many more, but every single one of them had one thing in common: the earth was supported by some visible, tangible thing. But God way back then used Job to tell us that the earth is hung on nothing. When did man finally figure that out? Look to a guy named Copernicus, around A.D. 1500.

Thousands of years before modern astronomers changed the world's view of this, the book of Job put it in writing. How did this old book get it right? God did that.

Here is another one:

Job 38:16 *Hast thou entered into the springs of the sea? or hast thou walked in the search of the depth?*

Way back then God spoke of springs in the sea. It took man another three thousand nine hundred years to build equipment good enough to go down and find them, and sure enough, they are there.

The book of Job will not likely ever shake an honest person's faith. What it will do is provide fodder for the skeptics who have already decided to disbelieve before they even examine the evidence. But in so doing they become the most ironic and pitiable of creatures: people who disbelieve God and what He said because of Job, when Job himself never ceased to believe in either.

Chapter Ten
A Bald Head and the Bear Truth

Let me give you a quote, with all of the filthy language bleeped out, and see if you recognize what the guy is talking about:

"So a guy named Eliseus was traveling to Bethel when a bunch of kids popped up and made fun of him for being bald. That had to _____, and you can't blame Eliseus for being _____ and cursing them to God. But God had Elisha's back, by which I mean he sent two bears to maul 42 of these kids to death. For making fun of a bald dude. I have to think Eliseus was looking for something along the lines of a spanking, or maybe the poetic justice of having the kids go bald, but nope, God went straight for the bear murder. But on the plus side, that pile of 40+ children's corpses never made fun of anybody again." (kenyatalk.com)

2 Kings 2:23 *And he went up from thence unto Bethel: and as he was going up by the way, there came forth little children out of the city, and mocked him, and said unto him, Go up, thou bald head; go up, thou bald head.* **24** *And he turned back, and looked on them, and cursed them in the name of the LORD. And there came forth two she bears out of* *the wood, and tare forty and two children of them.* **25** *And he went from thence to mount Carmel, and from thence he returned to Samaria.*

In most of these things I cover, if there is a jaw-dropping kind of revelation, I save it till last. In this instance, I am going to reverse that pattern, for a reason. We are, by nature, so protective of children that, if I do not deal with that aspect up front, there is likely to be some part of you deep inside not really paying attention to anything else I have to say. So let us deal right off the bat with the main target of the scoffers in this passage.

The age of the children

As you heard or read the above quote from an internet scoffer, it is very clear what he believes on this issue. He believes that forty-two little kids, maybe seven or eight years old, were killed by two bears. And that is exactly why the command of 2 Timothy 2:15 is so incredibly important:

2 Timothy 2:15 *Study to shew thyself approved unto God, a workman that needeth not to be ashamed, rightly dividing the word of truth.*

The Bible is too important and too powerful to be handled lightly. Every word needs to be placed under a microscope and fully understood before we come to any conclusions about any passage.

In this case, the entire crux of the matter hinges on the word children. Even in twenty-first century America, it is incredibly often used by people who are far older and more mature than a seven or eight-year-old. Even the word baby does not always mean an infant. On multiple occasions over the past few years starting from the riots in Ferguson over the Michael Brown case, on down the line through the troubles in New York and Baltimore, eighteen and nineteen-year-olds out in the street rioting and looting and killing have been called "children," "misguided youth," and even "my babies" by their parents.

136

So how are we to find out with any reasonable certainty how old these children likely were?

The most logical way to begin is with a word study. We need to take the Hebrew word used for children and see of whom else it was used, and how old they were.

There are two words to consider. The first is "little." It is the Hebrew word *Qatan*, and it does not deal with size, it literally means "young as opposed to old." The second word is children, it is from the word n*a'ar*. And here is where things get fun. Let me show you some people who were described as n*a'ar*, which the text we are considering renders as children.

Before I give you the first example, let me ask you another question similar to the one I asked a few moments ago. What is the oldest age that you would ever refer to someone as a "lad?"

Genesis 22:1 *And it came to pass after these things, that God did tempt Abraham, and said unto him, Abraham: and he said, Behold, here I am.* **2** *And he said, Take now thy son, thine only son Isaac, whom thou lovest, and get thee into the land of Moriah; and offer him there for a burnt offering upon one of the mountains which I will tell thee of.* **3** *And Abraham rose up early in the morning, and saddled his ass, and took two of his young men with him, and Isaac his son, and clave the wood for the burnt offering, and rose up, and went unto the place of which God had told him.* **4** *Then on the third day Abraham lifted up his eyes, and saw the place afar off.* **5** *And Abraham said unto his young men, Abide ye here with the ass; and I and the **lad** will go yonder and worship, and come again to you.*

That word "lad" in verse five is the same as the word used of the children in 2 Kings 2. But do you know how old Isaac was at this juncture? Most scholars say around 30 years old! When we think of the word lad we automatically think again of a little boy, but Isaac was an adult and still being

137

called a lad, and it is the exact same word used for children in 2 Kings 2.

Do I think that the children of 2 Kings 2 were thirty? Maybe not, but they absolutely were much older than most people think, and I will prove that to you shortly.

Here is another one:

Genesis 41:9 *Then spake the chief butler unto Pharaoh, saying, I do remember my faults this day:* **10** *Pharaoh was wroth with his servants, and put me in ward in the captain of the guard's house, both me and the chief baker:* **11** *And we dreamed a dream in one night, I and he; we dreamed each man according to the interpretation of his dream.* **12** *And there was there with us a young man, an Hebrew, servant to the captain of the guard; and we told him, and he interpreted to us our dreams; to each man according to his dream he did interpret.*

In verse twelve, the word for man is once again *na'ar*, the same as the word used for children in 2 Kings 2. But in this case, Joseph was thirty years old!

Here is another one:

1 Kings 20:13 *And, behold, there came a prophet unto Ahab king of Israel, saying, Thus saith the LORD, Hast thou seen all this great multitude? behold, I will deliver it into thine hand this day; and thou shalt know that I am the LORD.* **14** *And Ahab said, By whom? And he said, Thus saith the LORD, Even by the young men of the princes of the provinces. Then he said, Who shall order the battle? And he answered, Thou.*

In this case, soldiers getting ready to go out to battle are once again called *na'ar*, this time rendered "young men." So very clearly, this term, like the modern American uses of words like "children" and "youth" and even "babies" can mean something much older than what most people think. When my wife and I were in our early forties and had been married for twenty years, a dear lady up in her seventies who had been married for fifty years said, "You two are just babies!"

God called them little children, but He did not put an age on it, He did not even put an age range.

So, since the words "little children" in our text can mean anything from a kindergartner to what we today would consider a middle-aged man, we are going to have to look to the context of the passage to see if we can find some clues on their age.

Here is the passage again:

2 Kings 2:23 *And he went up from thence unto Bethel: and as he was going up by the way, there came forth little children out of the city, and mocked him, and said unto him, Go up, thou bald head; go up, thou bald head.* **24** *And he turned back, and looked on them, and cursed them in the name of the LORD. And there came forth two she bears out of the wood, and tare forty and two children of them.* **25** *And he went from thence to mount Carmel, and from thence he returned to Samaria.*

Let us notice several facts. First of all, there is a huge group of them, and they are coming out of the city limits, into the wilderness, which in those days was well known to be filled with ravenous beasts. But what do you not see? Parents! The only ones who came out of the city were these "children." If you have dozens and dozens of seven or eight-year-olds out of the city right near the edge of the woods, then you have dozens and dozens of parents nearby. And if you don't have dozens and dozens of parents, then you are not dealing with seven or eight-year-olds, you are likely dealing with something like seventeen or eighteen-year-olds.

Notice something else, specifically, what they said to him. Their insult was "Go up, thou bald head."

Pay very close attention. If they had said "the preacher is a baldy, the preacher is a baldy!" you might be dealing with seven- or eight-year-olds. But that isn't what they said. They began by saying the words "go up." What does that mean; to what does this refer? Here is the answer:

2 Kings 2:1 *And it came to pass, when the LORD would take up Elijah into heaven by a whirlwind, that Elijah went with Elisha from Gilgal.* **2** *And Elijah said unto Elisha, Tarry here, I pray thee; for the LORD hath sent me to Bethel. And Elisha said unto him, As the LORD liveth, and as thy soul liveth, I will not leave thee. So they went down to Bethel.* **3** *And the sons of the prophets that were at Bethel came forth to Elisha, and said unto him, Knowest thou that the LORD will take away thy master from thy head to day? And he said, Yea, I know it; hold ye your peace.* **4** *And Elijah said unto him, Elisha, tarry here, I pray thee; for the LORD hath sent me to Jericho. And he said, As the LORD liveth, and as thy soul liveth, I will not leave thee. So they came to Jericho.* **5** *And the sons of the prophets that were at Jericho came to Elisha, and said unto him, Knowest thou that the LORD will take away thy master from thy head to day? And he answered, Yea, I know it; hold ye your peace.* **6** *And Elijah said unto him, Tarry, I pray thee, here; for the LORD hath sent me to Jordan. And he said, As the LORD liveth, and as thy soul liveth, I will not leave thee. And they two went on.* **7** *And fifty men of the sons of the prophets went, and stood to view afar off: and they two stood by Jordan.* **8** *And Elijah took his mantle, and wrapped it together, and smote the waters, and they were divided hither and thither, so that they two went over on dry ground.* **9** *And it came to pass, when they were gone over, that Elijah said unto Elisha, Ask what I shall do for thee, before I be taken away from thee. And Elisha said, I pray thee, let a double portion of thy spirit be upon me.* **10** *And he said, Thou hast asked a hard thing: nevertheless, if thou see me when I am taken from thee, it shall be so unto thee; but if not, it shall not be so.* **11** *And it came to pass, as they still went on, and talked, that, behold, there appeared a chariot of fire, and horses of fire, and parted them both asunder; and Elijah* **went up** *by a whirlwind into heaven.* **12**

And Elisha saw it, and he cried, My father, my father, the chariot of Israel, and the horsemen thereof. And he saw him no more: and he took hold of his own clothes, and rent them in two pieces.

When they told Elisha to "go up," they were referring to what had just happened to Elijah. In doing so, they were saying, "We didn't like Elijah, and we don't like you, and since he just ascended up into heaven, why don't you go right on up with him!"

In other words, these "children" were old enough to be attempting to engage Elisha in a theological debate. They were old enough to see and realize what had just happened to Elijah, they were old enough to already be hardened against Elijah, and they were old enough to turn their hardness and mockery from Elijah to Elisha.

These "little children" were not young and innocent. They were old enough to clearly know right from wrong, and they were old enough to have already grown hard and sarcastic.

So, is "little children" a "bad translation?" No, of course not. It is not the Bible that needs fixing; it is our understanding that needs fixing. And what needs to be fixed in this case is the fact that we just normally assume everything from the standpoint of a twenty-first century American not realizing that our assumptions may be a mile off base. We think of little children as tykes and toddlers, but under certain circumstances, people in the Bible thought of twenty and thirty-year-olds as little children. But I am still not done yet. It would be enough, I think, just to point out that these "little children" likely were not nearly as young as you think. Now let me drop a bomb that dwarfs even that: no little children were even attacked by any bears!

You say, "Wait a minute, right there in verse twenty-three is says 'little children!'" Yes, it does. It says that little children came and mocked Elisha. But please show me where it says that "little children" were assaulted by the bears? Does it say that? No. What does it say and where?

2 Kings 2:24 *And he turned back, and looked on them, and cursed them in the name of the LORD. And there came forth two she bears out of the wood, and tare forty and two children of them.*

What difference do you notice between verse twenty-three and verse twenty-four? You read of little children in verse twenty-three, but the word little is left out of verse twenty-four. That is not an accident. In fact, even the word children is different in those two verses. Earlier it was the word *na'ar*. But in verse twenty-four it is the word *yeled*. That word simply means "a son or an offspring."

How many of you have a child in his forties or fifties? Do you change his diaper and burp him and take him to school every morning? No? Why? Because your child is actually grown. He is still a child, but he is not young anymore.

Why would God change words like that? Specifically to point out that He did NOT cause a bear to kill little tykes and toddlers! Little children came out to mock, yes, but when those bears rolled out of the woods, it was not *little* children that were attacked, it was just *children!*

You should know God well enough to know that He does what He does very exactly. And in this case, it was not babes and toddlers who, after innocently teasing, were destroyed haphazardly by bears. It was a huge group of people, some young, some older, and the older ones, the ones who knew better and were deciding to do wrong for themselves, were judged.

The agony of Elisha

For all of the false concern the scoffers demonstrate over these children, (and I say "false concern" because they do not actually believe that any of this ever happened, and thus their concern is merely a facade, a vehicle to be used to try and run God down in the streets) they are careful not to mention the agony of Elisha, mostly because they hate preachers.

Elisha had a close relationship with Elijah. How close? Look at how he regarded him:

2 Kings 2:11 *And it came to pass, as they still went on, and talked, that, behold, there appeared a chariot of fire, and horses of fire, and parted them both asunder; and Elijah went up by a whirlwind into heaven. 12 And Elisha saw it, and he cried,* **My father, my father,** *the chariot of Israel, and the horsemen thereof. And he saw him no more: and he took hold of his own clothes, and rent them in two pieces.*

Elijah was like a father to Elisha. Elisha had left his own father and mother behind to follow and serve Elijah. Elijah had poured his life into Elisha; he was the most influential person in his life.

And now he has lost him.

No matter how it happens, by death or by a miracle like this, it still hurts, and you would still miss him. To make matters worse, some well-meaning people have thrown uncertainty into the mix:

2 Kings 2:15 *And when the sons of the prophets which were to view at Jericho saw him, they said, The spirit of Elijah doth rest on Elisha. And they came to meet him, and bowed themselves to the ground before him. 16 And they said unto him, Behold now, there be with thy servants fifty strong men; let them go, we pray thee, and seek thy master: lest peradventure the Spirit of the LORD hath taken him up, and cast him upon some mountain, or into some valley. And he said, Ye shall not send. 17 And when they urged him till he was ashamed, he said, Send. They sent therefore fifty men; and they sought three days, but found him not. 18 And when they came again to him, (for he tarried at Jericho,) he said unto them, Did I not say unto you, Go not?*

Put yourself in his place. You have lost the most important person in the world to you, and suddenly someone comes and says, "They may not really be gone. Maybe there was some mistake..."

Then for the next three days, over your objections, they are out there trying to prove that there may have been a mistake!

Elisha is a man in agony, and no one is making it better. Even those that love him are actually making it worse. And it is then that he goes to a very special place and has something not so special happen:

2 Kings 2:23 *And he went up from thence unto Bethel: and as he was going up by the way, there came forth little children out of the city, and mocked him, and said unto him, Go up, thou bald head; go up, thou bald head.*

When you see the name Bethel, what in Scripture comes to mind? Bethel means "the house of God." Let me show you the first time it is mentioned in Scripture:

Genesis 12:8 *And he removed from thence unto a mountain on the east of Bethel, and pitched his tent, having Bethel on the west, and Hai on the east: and there he builded an altar unto the LORD, and called upon the name of the LORD.*

This passage is the account of Abraham. The very first time we see Bethel in the Bible was when Abraham built an altar there to worship the Lord. Bethel was a very special place to God and to His people. Look at what God said:

Genesis 31:13 *I am the God of Bethel, where thou anointedst the pillar, and where thou vowedst a vow unto me: now arise, get thee out from this land, and return unto the land of thy kindred.*

Bethel is mentioned over and over in verses like this. But by the time of Elisha things were in a bad state. You see, something had happened a few years back:

1 Kings 12:26 *And Jeroboam said in his heart, Now shall the kingdom return to the house of David: 27 If this people go up to do sacrifice in the house of the LORD at Jerusalem, then shall the heart of this people turn again unto* *their lord, even unto Rehoboam king of Judah, and they shall kill me, and go again to Rehoboam king of Judah.* **28** *Whereupon the king took counsel, and made two calves of gold, and said unto them, It is too much for you to go up to Jerusalem: behold thy gods, O Israel, which brought thee up out of the land of Egypt.* **29** *And he set the one in Bethel, and the other put he in Dan.*

King Jeroboam put a golden calf, an idol, in one of the holiest and most precious places to God in the land, Bethel. It was still there during the time of Elisha. It was not all that was there, though, the text tells us that there was also a school of the prophets. So, in the days of Elisha, there was a power struggle in Bethel. Look at what Matthew Henry said:

> "At Bethel there was another school of prophets. Thither Elisha went next, in this his primary visitation, and the scholars there no doubt welcomed him with all possible respect, but the townsmen were abusive to him. One of Jeroboam's calves was at Bethel; this they were proud of, and fond of, and hated those that reproved them. The law did not empower them to suppress this pious academy, but we may suppose it was their usual practice to jeer the prophets as they went along the streets, to call them by some nickname or other, that they might expose them to contempt, prejudice their youth against them, and, if possible, drive them out of their town." (2:718)

What happened to Elisha on this day was that he, as the new representative of God now that Elijah was gone, came under attack by followers of the golden calf worship of Jeroboam. These were not just kids tossing around a silly insult; these were idol worshipers challenging the prophet of God, and at the worst possible time for him, when he was at his very lowest!

But there is even another aspect to it, that of the bald head. Listen to Jamison, Fausset, and Brown:

"(this was) an epithet of contempt in the East, applied to a person even with a bushy head of hair." (1:375)

In other words, Elisha may not even have necessarily been bald; "bald head" was an insult. In the east, it was a sign of incredible shame to be bald, and "bald head" became a really filthy insult used to denote someone whose head, whose brain, was worthless. They were calling him an idiot!

The assault of the bears

2 Kings 2:23 *And he went up from thence unto Bethel: and as he was going up by the way, there came forth little children out of the city, and mocked him, and said unto him, Go up, thou bald head; go up, thou bald head.* **24** *And he turned back, and looked on them, and cursed them in the name of the LORD. And there came forth two she bears out of the wood, and tare forty and two children of them.*

Now that you are in the habit of reading and thinking rather than assuming, let me ask you a question. Did bears kill forty-two people in this text?

The quote I gave you from a scoffer says yes. He even used the word "corpses." But do you see the word "kill?" Do you even see the word "destroy?" Do you see the word he uses, the word corpses? No. But what word do you see? Tare. The spelling is different, but what does the word tare (tear) mean? It means to tear, to split, to rip.

Let me ask you a question. Is it possible for someone to be killed by being torn by a bear? Yes, certainly. But let me ask you another question. Is it possible for a person to survive being torn by a bear? Yes, it happens all the time. Watch the discovery channel, you will see interviews constantly by people who have been torn by bears, sharks, lions, etc. and lived to tell about it.

So the fact of the matter is, not only was it not tykes and toddlers assaulted by a bear, even those who were judged by this bear attack may not have even been killed! You have to *assume* something to come to the conclusion that they were killed.

Should we have a problem with it if they were? No. If God thought these forty-two needed it, and He Himself did it, He is just in His doings.

But we do not know for sure that so much as a single person died, and we most certainly do know that there were **not** forty-two corpses of little children laying there.

And that is just *A Bald Head And The Bear Truth*...

Chapter Eleven
Does God Tempt People or Not?

Before we turn to the Old Testament, let me show you a verse from the New Testament:

James 1:13 *Let no man say when he is tempted, I am tempted of God: for God cannot be tempted with evil, neither tempteth he any man:* **14** *But every man is tempted, when he is drawn away of his own lust, and enticed.*

Now with that verse in mind, let's look at one of the most familiar passages of the Old Testament, Genesis 22.

Genesis 22:1 *And it came to pass after these things, that God did tempt Abraham, and said unto him, Abraham: and he said, Behold, here I am.* **2** *And he said, Take now thy son, thine only son Isaac, whom thou lovest, and get thee into the land of Moriah; and offer him there for a burnt offering upon one of the mountains which I will tell thee of.* **3** *And Abraham rose up early in the morning, and saddled his ass, and took two of his young men with him, and Isaac his son, and clave the wood for the burnt offering, and rose up, and went unto the place of which God had told him.* **4** *Then on the third day Abraham lifted up his eyes, and saw the place afar off.* **5** *And Abraham said unto his young men, Abide ye here with the ass; and I and the lad will go yonder and worship, and come again to you.* **6** *And Abraham took the wood of the burnt offering, and laid it upon Isaac his son; and he took the fire in his hand, and a knife; and they went both of them* *together. 7 And Isaac spake unto Abraham his father, and said, My father: and he said, Here am I, my son. And he said, Behold the fire and the wood: but where is the lamb for a burnt offering? 8 And Abraham said, My son, God will provide himself a lamb for a burnt offering: so they went both of them together. 9 And they came to the place which God had told him of; and Abraham built an altar there, and laid the wood in order, and bound Isaac his son, and laid him on the altar upon the wood. 10 And Abraham stretched forth his hand, and took the knife to slay his son. 11 And the angel of the LORD called unto him out of heaven, and said, Abraham, Abraham: and he said, Here am I. 12 And he said, Lay not thine hand upon the lad, neither do thou any thing unto him: for now I know that thou fearest God, seeing thou hast not withheld thy son, thine only son from me. 13 And Abraham lifted up his eyes, and looked, and behold behind him a ram caught in a thicket by his horns: and Abraham went and took the ram, and offered him up for a burnt offering in the stead of his son. 14 And Abraham called the name of that place Jehovahjireh: as it is said to this day, In the mount of the LORD it shall be seen. 15 And the angel of the LORD called unto Abraham out of heaven the second time, 16 And said, By myself have I sworn, saith the LORD, for because thou hast done this thing, and hast not withheld thy son, thine only son: 17 That in blessing I will bless thee, and in multiplying I will multiply thy seed as the stars of the heaven, and as the sand which is upon the sea shore; and thy seed shall possess the gate of his enemies; 18 And in thy seed shall all the nations of the earth be blessed; because thou hast obeyed my voice. 19 So Abraham returned unto his young men, and they rose up and went together to Beersheba; and Abraham dwelt at Beersheba.*

This is one of the most glorious passages in the Old Testament, and one of the passages most hated by the devil because of what it represents. Because of that, it has always been a target for scoffers and skeptics, a battering ram used against the Old Testament, the God of the Old Testament, and the Bible as a whole. So, let us dig into it and see what there is to see.

A qualification of temptation

The very first thing we want to deal with is this issue of temptation. Let me begin by asking you a question: are you gay?

Gay is one word, but it has multiple definitions. Its original meaning was "happy." Now it normally means homosexual. You are going to have to watch how it is used in context to determine what it means.

For instance, in the context of the "fa la la la la" Christmas song:

Don we now our gay apparel...

What does that mean? Happy, festive, happy looking.

But in the context of the modern culture, if some man stands up and says "I'm gay!" what does that mean?

Words have always been like that; defined both by word and by context. Temptation is exactly like that. It has not one but two primary meanings in the Bible. The first is "a solicitation to do evil." Think in terms of a prostitute trying to lure in a married man. The second, though, is "a trial or testing."

Let me give you several verses with temptation and related words, and you see if you can figure out what it means in each verse.

Matthew 26:41 *Watch and pray, that ye enter not into temptation: the spirit indeed is willing, but the flesh is weak.*

This is pretty clearly a solicitation to sin. But here is another one:

James 1:2 *My brethren, count it all joy when ye fall into divers temptations;*

Pray tell, do you think for even a moment that this means "a solicitation to sin?"

151

"My brethren count it all joy when your neighbor's wife asks you to commit adultery with her... count it all joy when you are given the opportunity to murder someone you are angry with... count it all joy when your flesh craves liquor and drugs..."

Clearly, that is not what the word temptation means in that verse. To further verify that, look at the very next verse:

James 1:3 *Knowing this, that the trying of your faith worketh patience.*

Verse three defines the terms of verse two. The temptation spoken of in verse two is not a solicitation to sin, it is a trial of faith. Peter used the word the exact same way:

1 Peter 1:6 *Wherein ye greatly rejoice, though now for a season, if need be, ye are in heaviness through manifold* **temptations***: 7 That* **the trial of your faith***, being much more precious than of gold that perisheth, though it be tried with fire, might be found unto praise and honour and glory at the appearing of Jesus Christ:*

There are a great many instances in the Bible of the word temptation being used as a solicitation to sin, and there are also a great many instances in the Bible of it being used in the sense of a trial or testing.

A person struggling with pornography is being tempted. But so is a person who has just been told he or she has cancer.

A person desperately wanting to tell a lie is being tempted. But so is a person who is struggling to make ends meet and wondering if God will come through.

Temptation can be either a solicitation to sin or a trial or test. And when it comes to our text in Genesis 22 compared to our text in James 1:13-14, God was very kind to actually define something for us. Look at it once again:

James 1:13 *Let no man say when he is tempted, I am tempted of God: for God cannot be tempted* **with evil***, neither tempteth he any man: 14 But every man is tempted, when he is drawn away of his own lust, and enticed.*

That phrase "with evil" lets us know what kind of tempting God never does. He Himself cannot be tempted with evil, He cannot be solicited to sin, and He also will not ever use that kind of temptation on man. So, each and every time we see the word temptation used in regard to God's dealing with man, it will never be the first kind of temptation; it will always be the second. It will never be a solicitation to evil; it will always be a trial or test.

So, when Genesis 22:1 says:

Genesis 22:1 *And it came to pass after these things, that God did **tempt** Abraham...*

It means that He came to Abraham with a trial, a test. There is no contradiction between the two passages. God did not intend to get Abraham to do something wrong, He intended to test his faith. Look what Hebrews 11:6 says about this:

Hebrews 11:17 *By faith Abraham, when he was **tried**, offered up Isaac:*

There is absolute confirmation of how we are to take that word "tempted" in Genesis 22:1. God did not tempt Abraham with evil, He tried, He tested him.

A quandary of a request

Genesis 22:1 *And it came to pass after these things, that God did tempt Abraham, and said unto him, Abraham: and he said, Behold, here I am. **2** And he said, Take now thy son, thine only son Isaac, whom thou lovest, and get thee into the land of Moriah; and offer him there for a burnt offering upon one of the mountains which I will tell thee of.*

Right at the outset, let us dispel a faulty notion since facts often repaint the entire picture. Most people assume, and most paintings show prime of life, healthy and strong Abraham raising up his knife over a little boy getting ready to kill him. But the truth is the exact opposite; Abraham by this point was around 130, and Isaac around 30. Now please tell me something, if a 130-year-old is going to sacrifice a 30-

year-old, what is going to have to be the case concerning that 30-year-old? He is going to have to be a willing participant!

When verse nine says that Abraham bound his son upon the altar, Isaac had to let him do it. There is no way in the world a young and healthy 30-year-old is going to be overpowered by an ancient 130-year-old.

With that established, please understand that this was still a huge quandary of a request.

It was a huge quandary because this son Isaac had already been specifically stated by God to be the chosen seed, the one who would bear grandchildren to Abraham, leading to great-grandchildren, and great-great-grandchildren until they became the world's most important nation. And yet here is God, already having said that, telling Abraham to sacrifice his son. That is a quandary of a request!

It was also a huge quandary because based on what Abraham knew of God's character, this seemed to be un-understandable. The heathen gods all around him demanded human sacrifice, but the God that spoke to Abraham had always been radically different. That makes this a quandary of a request!

You and I know that God was not going to let him go through with it, but Abraham thought that He was.

You say, "That makes him a terrible father!" No, it does not, and I will explain why in just a bit.

A question of omniscience

Fast forward with me to the end of the account for a few moments. Here is something else the scoffers love to pound on:

Genesis 22:10 *And Abraham stretched forth his hand, and took the knife to slay his son.* **11** *And the angel of the LORD called unto him out of heaven, and said, Abraham, Abraham: and he said, Here am I.* **12** *And he said, Lay not thine hand upon the lad, neither do thou any thing unto him:*

154

for now I know that thou fearest God, *seeing thou hast not withheld thy son, thine only son from me.*

You will not have any trouble figuring out what the scoffer loves about this. "You call God omniscient? You say He knows everything? He did not even know if Abraham feared Him! He had to lay out this elaborate test to figure it out!"

To say that is to insert something into Scripture that is not there. God did not say, "I did not know, but now I do," He simply said, "For now I know." You can know something now that you have known before. You can speak in terms of the here and now without meaning anything about the past.

There have been many, many, many times when God has done something very good for me, and in response, I have said, "Boy, now I KNOW that God is good!" Did I not know it before? Of course. But another experience had shown me again what I already previously knew.

Yes, God already knew that Abraham feared Him. But now He knew it all over again based on the present actions of Abraham.

Something you need to know about your Bible is that since God wrote it to us, He often speaks from our perspective. Here is an example:

Genesis 15:12 *And when the sun was going down, a deep sleep fell upon Abram; and, lo, an horror of great darkness fell upon him.*

It is this kind of a phrase in the Bible that the critic loves to pounce on and say, "Aha! See? You can't trust your Bible because the sun doesn't actually go down! Modern science has proven that it stays put, and the earth rotates, thus making it appear that it goes down and rises!"

But wait a minute; who else do you know that every morning tells the entire area what time "sundown" is going to be? That would be the weatherman. What is he doing? The same thing God does in the Bible, speaking to us from our perspective.

When you see things like God asking Adam and Eve where they were, or saying, "Now I know" to Abraham, it is not a proof that He is not omniscient, it is a proof that He loves us enough to speak to us in terms that are familiar to us.

And as we continue on, we will find that it was the very omniscience of God that led Him to do everything He did on this day. He did not "learn something that He never knew." He did some things to teach us what we needed to know. Let's keep going, and I will show you what I mean.

Genesis 22:2 *And he said, Take now thy son, thine only son Isaac, whom thou lovest, and get thee into the land of* **Moriah***; and offer him there for a burnt offering upon* **one of the mountains which I will tell thee of.**

Genesis 22:9 *And they came to* **the place which God had told him of***; and Abraham built an altar there, and laid the wood in order, and bound Isaac his son, and laid him on the altar upon the wood.*

As Abraham made his way on a long three-day journey, it was not to some general, random location. There was one very specific place that God had in mind. We see that it was on a mountain, and we find the name of the land that the mountain was in was called Moriah. We then find in verse nine that there was one specific place in that land that God had in mind.

The Old Testament calls it by the name Moriah. In the land of Moriah there was a mountain also called Moriah. It was on that mount that Solomon's temple later sat. The summit of that mountain called Moriah in the land then called Moriah by the time of the New Testament had a name that we are very familiar with:

Luke 23:33 *And when they were come to the place, which is called* **Calvary***, there they crucified him, and the malefactors, one on the right hand, and the other on the left.*

When Abraham took his son up Moriah, he was taking him up a mountain whose summit would one day be called Calvary. And God did not just direct him to the mountain, He

156

directed him to a particular spot on the mountain. As perfect of a picture as God paints, you will never convince me that Abraham put that altar anywhere other than the exact spot where an old rugged cross would one day stand!

Genesis 22:11 *And the angel of the LORD called unto him out of heaven, and said, Abraham, Abraham: and he said, Here am I.* **12** *And he said, Lay not thine hand upon the lad, neither do thou any thing unto him: for now I know that thou fearest God, seeing thou hast not withheld thy son, thine only son from me.* **13** *And Abraham lifted up his eyes, and looked, and behold behind him a ram caught in a thicket by his horns: and Abraham went and took the ram, and offered him up for a burnt offering in the stead of his son.* **14** *And Abraham called the name of that place Jehovahjireh: as it is said to this day, In the mount of the LORD it shall be seen.*

On that mountain on that day, a father and a son agreed on a sacrifice. The father initiated it, the son willingly laid down to allow it. This is the utterly perfect picture of God the Father and God the Son agreeing on the Son's crucifixion to pay for the sin debt of all mankind.

Right before Abraham took his son's life, God called to him audibly. He stopped Abraham from doing what he had intended to do, and it was then that Abraham lifted up his eyes and saw a ram caught in a thicket by his horns. How odd that a creature like that would end up caught like that! But God was providing a sacrifice for Himself just as Abraham had told Isaac that he would in verse eight.

Abraham sacrificed that ram instead, and he and Isaac went back down the mountain together. All of this was the omniscience of God on full display.

He knew what Abraham would do with this test.

He knew that He Himself would one day sacrifice His Own Son on that spot and that this time the Son would not be given a substitute, the Son would be the substitute.

He knew that a ram would be needed for Abraham, and so He sent one.

A quintessential faith

I believe we have cleared the reputation of God quite nicely as if that is even needed! God did not solicit Abraham to sin, He tested his faith, He put him through a trial. God did not do this so that He could figure out if Abraham really feared Him; He already knew that. He just spoke in terms we could understand. He was not being haphazard and cruel; He was painting the most vivid picture possible of the fact the He would one day send His Own Son up that hill to die.

But we still, I think, need to say some things about Abraham. What are we to make of his decision to sacrifice his son?

Let us establish some facts to work with as a foundation.

Fact number one: God promised that Isaac would marry and bear children, and he had not yet done so.

Fact number two: God was now telling Abraham to kill him.

Fact number three: dead people do not marry and bear children!

The facts before us give us a simple logic test, really. Many years ago, Sir Arthur Conan Doyle, author and creator of Sherlock Holmes, said, "Once you eliminate the impossible, whatever remains, no matter how improbable, must be the truth."

The "impossible" in this equation is the possibility of dead people marrying and bearing children. There is something else the Bible tells us is impossible. Hebrews 6:18 tells us that it is impossible for God to lie. Abraham knew both of those things, so he eliminated the impossible, and then believed the improbable. So what is it that Abraham believed concerning all of this?

Hebrews 11:17 *By faith Abraham, when he was tried, offered up Isaac: and he that had received the promises offered up his only begotten son,* **18** *Of whom it was said, That in Isaac shall thy seed be called:* **19** *Accounting that*

God was able to raise him up, even from the dead; from whence also he received him in a figure.

Abraham believed that God was going to have Isaac marry and bear children, he believed that God wanted him to sacrifice Isaac, and therefore the conclusion that he came to was that God was going to raise him from the dead! Look back in Genesis 22 at what he told the men who went on the journey with him:

Genesis 22:5 *And Abraham said unto his young men, Abide ye here with the ass; and I and the lad will go yonder and worship, and come again to you.*

Having audibly heard the voice of God tell him that Isaac would marry and bear children, he believed it. Having audibly heard the voice of God telling him to sacrifice Isaac, he then came to the only conclusion that made any sense to him based on what he already knew of the character of God: God was going to immediately raise him from the dead! They were going to go up onto the mountain together, he was going to sacrifice his son, and then he and his son were coming right back down.

And now a word of warning: God never before or since asked anyone anything like this. And God is not speaking audibly now; He has given us His written word to live by. God is never again going to say anything like this to anyone, so don't go joining some doomsday cult. But what you should learn from this passage is that God did right, and Abraham did right, and it all turned out right. You can trust the God of the Old Testament who is also the God of the New Testament. God was and is omniscient, and the plan of God was always, always, always the cross.

Chapter Twelve
Forbidden Fruit and Free Will

Genesis 3:1 *Now the serpent was more subtil than any beast of the field which the LORD God had made. And he said unto the woman, Yea, hath God said, Ye shall not eat of every tree of the garden?* **2** *And the woman said unto the serpent, We may eat of the fruit of the trees of the garden:* **3** *But of the fruit of the tree which is in the midst of the garden, God hath said, Ye shall not eat of it, neither shall ye touch it, lest ye die.* **4** *And the serpent said unto the woman, Ye shall not surely die:* **5** *For God doth know that in the day ye eat thereof, then your eyes shall be opened, and ye shall be as gods, knowing good and evil.* **6** *And when the woman saw that the tree was good for food, and that it was pleasant to the eyes, and a tree to be desired to make one wise, she took of the fruit thereof, and did eat, and gave also unto her husband with her; and he did eat.* **7** *And the eyes of them both were opened, and they knew that they were naked; and they sewed fig leaves together, and made themselves aprons.* **8** *And they heard the voice of the LORD God walking in the garden in the cool of the day: and Adam and his wife hid themselves from the presence of the LORD God amongst the trees of the garden.* **9** *And the LORD God called unto Adam, and said unto him, Where art thou?* **10** *And he said, I heard thy voice in the garden, and I was afraid, because I was naked; and I hid myself.* **11** *And he said, Who told thee that thou wast* *naked? Hast thou eaten of the tree, whereof I commanded thee that thou shouldest not eat?* **12** *And the man said, The woman whom thou gavest to be with me, she gave me of the tree, and I did eat.* **13** *And the LORD God said unto the woman, What is this that thou hast done? And the woman said, The serpent beguiled me, and I did eat.* **14** *And the LORD God said unto the serpent, Because thou hast done this, thou art cursed above all cattle, and above every beast of the field; upon thy belly shalt thou go, and dust shalt thou eat all the days of thy life:* **15** *And I will put enmity between thee and the woman, and between thy seed and her seed; it shall bruise thy head, and thou shalt bruise his heel.* **16** *Unto the woman he said, I will greatly multiply thy sorrow and thy conception; in sorrow thou shalt bring forth children; and thy desire shall be to thy husband, and he shall rule over thee.* **17** *And unto Adam he said, Because thou hast hearkened unto the voice of thy wife, and hast eaten of the tree, of which I commanded thee, saying, Thou shalt not eat of it: cursed is the ground for thy sake; in sorrow shalt thou eat of it all the days of thy life;* **18** *Thorns also and thistles shall it bring forth to thee; and thou shalt eat the herb of the field;* **19** *In the sweat of thy face shalt thou eat bread, till thou return unto the ground; for out of it wast thou taken: for dust thou art, and unto dust shalt thou return.* **20** *And Adam called his wife's name Eve; because she was the mother of all living.* **21** *Unto Adam also and to his wife did the LORD God make coats of skins, and clothed them.* **22** *And the LORD God said, Behold, the man is become as one of us, to know good and evil: and now, lest he put forth his hand, and take also of the tree of life, and eat, and live for ever:* **23** *Therefore the LORD God sent him forth from the garden of Eden, to till the ground from whence he was taken.* **24** *So he drove out the man; and he placed at the east of the garden of Eden Cherubims, and a flaming sword which turned every way, to keep the way of the tree of life.*

Genesis 4:1 *And Adam knew Eve his wife; and she conceived, and bare Cain, and said, I have gotten a man from the LORD. 2 And she again bare his brother Abel. And Abel was a keeper of sheep, but Cain was a tiller of the ground. 3 And in process of time it came to pass, that Cain brought of the fruit of the ground an offering unto the LORD. 4 And Abel, he also brought of the firstlings of his flock and of the fat thereof. And the LORD had respect unto Abel and to his offering: 5 But unto Cain and to his offering he had not respect. And Cain was very wroth, and his countenance fell. 6 And the LORD said unto Cain, Why art thou wroth? and why is thy countenance fallen? 7 If thou doest well, shalt thou not be accepted? and if thou doest not well, sin lieth at the door. And unto thee shall be his desire, and thou shalt rule over him. 8 And Cain talked with Abel his brother: and it came to pass, when they were in the field, that Cain rose up against Abel his brother, and slew him.*

"Never shall I forget that night, the first night in camp, which has turned my life into one long night, seven times cursed and seven times sealed. Never shall I forget that smoke. Never shall I forget the little faces of the children, whose bodies I saw turned into wreaths of smoke beneath a silent blue sky. Never shall I forget those flames which consumed my faith forever. Never shall I forget that nocturnal silence which deprived me, for all eternity, of the desire to live. Never shall I forget those moments which murdered my God and my soul and turned my dreams to dust. Never shall I forget these things, even if I am condemned to live as long as God Himself. Never." Elie Wiesel, Holocaust survivor, noted author, from the book "Night." (34)

If there is any question that consumes the thoughts of both lost and saved as they consider the God they either believe in or vehemently deny, it is the question of why a good God would allow such great suffering in the world.

Six million Jews brutally murdered by the Nazi's, including Elie Wiesel's mother, father, and younger sister...

Hundreds of precious little girls kidnaped by Muslims under the name Boko Haram and raped over and over for months...

Tens of millions of Russians murdered under Joseph Stalin. We always hear that religion is the source of all evil in the world, but there has never been more bloodshed, anywhere, ever, than under the atheism of Russia, Stalin, and the Soviet Union...

Every new day brings news stories of atrocities, murders, unspeakable cruelty and violence. And each time we look either at the past or the present and see such things, it is inevitable that our thoughts turn to an all-powerful God who could stop it all but does not.

This raises questions, legitimate questions. Here is a basic summary of those questions:

If there is a God who, because of His omnipotence, could stop all of it and yet does not, does He not then become responsible for it?

If there is a God who, because of His omniscience, could have prevented all of it, does He not then become responsible for it?

If God from time to time intervenes, miraculously saving a person or two, is He not playing favorites? And if He can do it for some, He could clearly do it for all, so is He not wrong to only help a few?

Why would a good God allow bad things to happen to good people?

We will examine all of that in this chapter, and to do so, we will need to go back to the very beginning. You see, the critic does not find his way out into the middle of the Bible and then suddenly discover that he has a problem with

God. The critic has a problem with God from the very creation itself, right from Genesis 1:1 on out.

In our text verses from Genesis chapters three and four, we see the account of man falling into sin. Right after they did so, we are taken ahead in time to the very first murder as Cain killed his brother Abel. It took less than one generation after the first sin for people to start murdering each other, and things have not gotten any better since.

Think of 9/11 and tell me if things have gotten better.

Think once again of the Holocaust and tell me if things have gotten better.

Think of children that are abused in the worst ways by people they should be able to trust and tell me if things have gotten better.

So, to summarize the atheist view, "If God is real, and if He is good like you say, why would He allow all of this? You actually believe Genesis chapters one through three, you actually believe that God made man, knowing that he would fall. You actually believe that He knew the serpent would tempt Eve and that she would give in. You actually believe that God stood back somewhere while it happened. So, tell me, if all that is true, how can you call your God good?"

You will hear that line of argumentation over and over again. You will see scoffers tear into the first three chapters of Genesis in order to tear down God. So, what are we to learn, and how are we to deal with this? Let's handle this by asking and answering the questions we posed earlier.

If there is a God who, because of His omnipotence, could stop all of it (evil) and yet does not, does He not then become responsible for it?

Here is part one of the answer: how do you know that anything actually *is* evil?

Do you realize that by even asking the question you are stipulating to the fact that there is a God? This is exactly what brought a former atheist named C. S. Lewis to Christ. He said, "My argument against God was that the universe seemed so cruel and unjust. But how had I got this idea of just and unjust? A man does not call a line crooked unless he has some idea of a straight line. What was I comparing this universe with when I called it unjust?"

The scoffer responds, "Wait a minute, we don't need God to have right and wrong, we don't need God to know the difference between good and evil. We can decide that for ourselves!"

As I heard Ravi Zacharias say, "Sir, in some cultures people love their neighbors, in other cultures people eat their neighbors."

If we the people get to decide what is right and wrong, good and evil, then right and wrong and good and evil become nothing more than the whims of the moment. In Nazi Germany, it was considered right to slaughter six million Jews. In America two hundred years ago, it was considered right to own other human beings as slaves. In some cultures and religions, people still regard slavery as right.

If there is no standard outside of ourselves, then there literally is no such thing as evil, there are only "things that I don't personally like, that other people may personally like."

Furthermore, by using the term "evil," you have just stipulated to the fact that evolution is a lie. If we just sort of happened, if the universe burped and out popped us, and then we slowly evolved through the process known as "natural selection and survival of the fittest," then please tell me where exactly "evil" fits into that evolutionary framework? I would have a bit more respect for evolutionists if they would be consistent enough to only speak in terms of the material and never mention the moral because evolution does not have any room for the moral or even any mechanism to bring it into being.

If there is no God and evolution is true, then why do people feel guilty over getting by with whatever they can get by with because no matter what it is, it is not actually wrong! No one faults a Praying Mantis for eating her children; it is what nature has decreed. So why should anyone fault a human mother for eating her children? Why should anyone regard it as evil if we all crawled out of the same primordial ooze? We may be squeamish at it, we may personally not like it, but who are we to judge? Who are we to say "thus and so is evil" when someone else may feel differently about it?

The scoffer will tell every Christian to stop judging, and then will turn right around and ask why a good God would allow "evil" into the world, not even understanding that they are themselves then judging and giving testimony to the fact that there is an absolute moral law, and therefore an absolute moral lawgiver.

Let me give you the first question again, and then I will give you part two of the answer to it:

"If there is a God who because of His omnipotence could stop all of it (evil) and yet does not, does He not then become responsible for it?"

Part two of the answer to that first question is: Just on a logical level alone, the answer is no. Furthermore, the atheist/scoffer/liberal actually behaves much the same way they accuse God of behaving on this issue, yet they believe it is right!

Here is what I mean. Does the United States of America have the ability to intervene in conflicts around the world? Do we have the ability to put boots on the ground in Iraq, Afghanistan, Chechnya, Ukraine, Africa? Yes, we surely do! But have you ever known any atheist/scoffer/liberal who desired to do so? Not likely. They are usually the ones at the very forefront of telling people that we shouldn't be going to war to stop evil people from hurting innocent people; we should just mind our own business. But if God is evil because He does not use His power to stop evil, then we are evil every time we do not use our power to stop evil.

The fact is, evil is neither God's fault nor God's responsibility to stop. There was no evil among mankind until we, mankind, brought it into our midst by that first sin.

God made us a world free from any and all violence and hurt:

Genesis 1:31a *And God saw every thing that he had made, and, behold, it was very good.*

The fact that we took a world with no violence and no hurt in it and then corrupted it means that we are the ones responsible for violence and hurt, and we are the ones responsible for confronting it and dealing with it. Accusing God of being evil for not stopping the evil that we created and that we perpetuate makes us a lot like the U.S. government; make a mess and then pass the buck!

If there is a God who, because of His omniscience, could have prevented all of it, does He not then become responsible for it?

"But wait, wait, wait!" cries the scoffer. "You may have shown that the omnipotence of God does not make Him responsible for stopping all evil, but let's go back even further. The omnipotence of God may not make Him responsible, but the omniscience of God surely does! You yourself admit that He knew the devil would tempt us, He knew we were going to sin, He knew we were going to mess things up, and yet He made us anyway, and He allowed us to be tempted anyway. Ergo, God is at fault for the violence and hurt that people endure."

In order to deal with that faulty thinking, let us examine the only three possible options God had. Some may divide a couple of these three into a couple of more finely split options, but in its most basic sense, here are the options God had when it came to the creation of man:

One: Not make humans at all.

Two: Make humans, but deprive them of any free will, thus ensuring that they never sin.

Three: Make humans, and allow them a free will, knowing that they would sin.

I think we can all readily agree that none of us like the idea of option number one. This whole "existing" thing? It really is kind of nice, and none of us really want to do without it.

So, option number one is not one that mankind would choose.

Option number two is also one that none of us would like, especially not the atheist/scoffer/liberal. Do you really think that people who march in the streets demanding the right to smoke pot, "change their gender," engage in sodomy, watch pornography, and have liquor by the drink would be at all too keen on the idea of a righteous, pure, holy God moving them about like puppets on a string?

Do you think for a moment that any person like that would agree to being forced to go to church three times a week, being forced to tithe, being forced to worship, and being forced to be straight and pure and holy in their behavior?

This is the exact thing that none of them want, ever! Their attitude is still the same as Jesus described in Luke 19:14:

Luke 19:14 *But his citizens hated him, and sent a message after him, saying,* **We will not have this man to reign over us.**

Their attitude is still the same as the psalmist described in Psalm 2:1-3:

Psalm 2:1 *Why do the heathen rage, and the people imagine a vain thing?* **2** *The kings of the earth set themselves, and the rulers take counsel together, against the LORD, and against his anointed, saying,* **3** *Let us break their bands asunder, and cast away their cords from us.*

There is not an honest atheist in the world that would actually be okay with that second option. But that only leaves one option, the third option, the one where God makes man, gives him a free will, and then lets him choose.

"But wait, wait! What about the devil tempting man? How does that fit into your options?"

It fits perfectly, actually. Think about it: if man is never ever tempted to do wrong, then does he really have a free will? No! The only way man really has a free will is if he actually has real options and a real pull from both sides.

You see, God never wanted robots. He desired actual people with actual free wills and actual choices, people who would be wooed by God on the one hand, wooed by the devil on the other, and then freely chose God. Did He not know that Satan would win that first critical round, and that man would be plunged into sin? Certainly. And that allowed Him to woo us in the most profound way of all: literally, actually, physically "loving us to death..."

If God from time to time intervenes, miraculously saving a person or two, is He not playing favorites? And if He can do it for some, He could clearly do it for all, so is He not wrong to only help a few?

When you go back to that quote by the great Elie Weisel, it is just about impossible to not have your heart break. When you go through the Holocaust Museum and see an exhibit where a child is saying, "I prayed, and God did not answer," it will make you cry anguished tears.

But if you think it breaks your heart and makes you cry, imagine what it does to the heart of God! But you see, for the most part, the suffering and evil and violence of mankind against mankind actually serves a great purpose, one so great that God only very rarely interrupts it. Let me show you an example of that from Scripture, perhaps the most poignant example of all.

Luke 2:34 *And Simeon blessed them, and said unto Mary his mother, Behold, this child is set for the fall and rising again of many in Israel; and for a sign which shall be spoken against;* **35** *(Yea, a sword shall pierce through thy own soul also,) that the thoughts of many hearts may be revealed.*

This scene took place in the temple when Jesus was still a baby. Old Simeon spoke of the fact that Jesus would suffer immensely, but he also mentioned Mary's suffering. Here is where that prophecy was fulfilled:

John 19:25a *Now there stood by the cross of Jesus his mother...*

When you consider the suffering of Jesus, truly it was, in every regard, the worst suffering anyone has ever endured, because it combined the deepest physical suffering imaginable with the even greater suffering of Him becoming sin for all mankind! But one aspect of His suffering is especially relevant to our discussion, and that was the suffering of His mother.

Mary was being crushed, devastated, tortured. Her child, her son, was being crucified before her very eyes.

Do you not think that she prayed for it to stop?

Do you not think she cried out to God for a miracle?

And was a miracle available? Certainly:

Matthew 26:52 *Then said Jesus unto him, Put up again thy sword into his place: for all they that take the sword shall perish with the sword.* **53** *Thinkest thou that I cannot now pray to my Father, and he shall presently give me more than twelve legions of angels?* **54** *But how then shall the scriptures be fulfilled, that thus it must be?*

So a miracle was available, Mary's prayers could have been answered. But that suffering served too great a purpose for it to be stopped. Our salvation depended on it!

And it is the exact same way with all of the suffering that we see in the world that God chooses not to stop. In large measure, our salvation depends on it!

171

Think about it: how many people would ever accept the Lord as their Savior if we lived in a perfect, peaceful, sin-free world? Can you think of a number? The number is "zero."

It is suffering and pain and a wrecked and ruined world that makes us aware of our need for a Savior! Without suffering and pain, this entire world would be headed for an eternity of suffering and pain in Hell, because we would not even be aware that we are fallen and lost.

Pain serves a purpose: it lets us know that something is incredibly wrong and needs to be fixed:

A child was born with a rare congenital disease called CIPA (congenital insensitivity to pain with anhidrosis). This horrific disease has stricken only a very few people in human history. The body simply does not feel pain, but this does not mean that the body cannot be wounded. In fact, therein lies the danger: The girl could step on a rusty nail that penetrated her foot and consequently develop a life-threatening infection, but she would feel no pain and not even realize that she had been wounded. She could place her hand on a burning stove and not feel the flesh melt.

In an interview, her mother said, "My prayer for my daughter every night is, Dear God, please let my daughter be able to feel pain." (www.http://rzim.org/just-thinking/why-suffering-the-question)

Suffering serves a purpose, even suffering so great that we cannot possibly wrap our minds around it: it lets us know that something is incredibly wrong and needs to be fixed.

"But wait! Why then does God (according to YOU) sometimes do miracles and deliver people from evil and suffering? Is He not wrong for playing favorites?"

This is the question that I got hit with a few months ago when I mentioned to an atheist that God had been good to me. She said, "Oh how nice that God picked you as a favorite, while kids everywhere have to suffer!"

So, since God clearly can deliver, since He can do miracles, is He somehow playing favorites, is He somehow doing wrong?

In order to think that He is doing wrong, what you are really saying is that anything bad that ever happens to anyone makes God evil. In other words, you are right back to asserting that God has to exercise His omnipotence and put a stop to every evil. But once again, in so doing, He has just removed all pain from the equation and, therefore, removed any incentive for us to be saved and avoid Hell.

So why then does He ever do miracles? Why does He, every once in a great while, step in and save someone?

He did so for Elisha in 2 Kings 6, sending a mountain full of horse and chariots of fire to protect him.

He did so in Acts 12, sending an angel to spring Peter out of prison.

He did so in Genesis 19, dragging Lot out of Sodom.

He did so in A.D. 1384 for John Wycliffe, causing an earthquake just as he was headed for the stake.

God can miraculously deliver, and He sometimes does.

But do you know why miracles are so impressive and noticeable? Because they are so very rare, just like huge, flawless diamonds. If the entire surface of the earth was covered in huge, flawless diamonds, do you know what we would do with them? Yawn at them, ground them up, and pave roads with them.

Just like suffering, miracles serve a purpose. Suffering is designed to let us know something is wrong and needs to be fixed, miracles are designed to let us know there is a God who can fix it, and that we need to seek Him out.

If it was all suffering and no miracles, we would be hopeless, because we would not know there is a God who can help us. If it was all miracles and therefore no suffering, the entire world would be bright and cheery and blissfully happy as we slid off into hell by the millions.

But a wise and loving God allows us just enough suffering to conclusively prove to us that we, mankind, are evil to the core and in need of a Savior. And that very same wise and loving God allows us just enough miracles to let us know that He is and that He cares and that we need to seek Him out.

It would be very hard to rationally argue that mankind is inherently good in the light of such great evidence to the contrary as the Holocaust. And it would also be very hard to rationally argue that there is no hope for things to change in light of the Biblical and historical evidence of a God who sometimes does a miracle and delivers people from trouble.

But why would a good God allow bad things to happen to good people?

That question we largely answered just a moment ago. But it is worth our while to examine it again by itself for two very important reasons. One, it assumes a false premise, and two, it is backward in its focus.

The false premise it assumes is that there are such things as "good people." Before you reflexively recoil against that, please pay attention. There most certainly are "people that we love." There most certainly are "people who are young and tender and worthy of being protected."

But it is when we assign the word "good" to the equation that we have crossed a line we had no right to cross:

Mark 10:18 *And Jesus said unto him, Why callest thou me good? there is none good but one, that is, God.*

For the record, we know that Jesus was speaking rhetorically, not claiming that He was not God. But the point He made about mankind was literal, not rhetorical. Mankind, one and all, fell into sin along with Adam in that Garden:

Romans 5:12 *Wherefore, as by one man sin entered into the world, and death by sin; and so death passed upon all men, for that all have sinned:*

174

The old statement accurately goes "In Adam's fall, we sinned all!"

The Bible does not teach that everyone is as bad as he or she can be, but it does teach that everyone is as bad off as he or she can be. Every human being who has ever been born has been born lost and under the curse of sin. So when someone says, "Why would God allow bad things to happen to good people," the correct answer is "God has never, ever let anything bad happen to a good person, because there is no such thing as a good person."

And that is why His love for us is so amazing. If we were good, it would make sense that He loves us. But the Bible says:

Romans 5:8 *But God commendeth his love toward us, in that, while we were yet sinners, Christ died for us.*

And that brings us to the second problem with the question, the fact that it is backward in its focus. You see, we shouldn't so much be asking why God lets bad things happen to good people as we should be asking why God lets good things happen to bad people!

Do you know why the Holocaust and 9/11 stand out so much in people's minds? Things like that stand out in our minds because they are so rare. On a day to day basis and life to life basis, human beings experience far more of the goodness of God than they do the badness of man.

We live in a fallen, sin-cursed world, and yet God is still so good to all of us on a daily basis that He is able to say this:

Romans 2:4 *Or despisest thou the riches of his goodness and forbearance and longsuffering; not knowing that **the goodness of God leadeth thee to repentance?***

We should not be at all amazed when humanity experiences evil and hurt. What we should truly be amazed at is that according to **Matthew 5:45** *...he maketh his sun to rise on the evil and on the good, and sendeth rain on the just and on the unjust.*

Man ate the forbidden fruit. A good God gave him the free will to do so. And then He loved fallen man to death, His own death.

Chapter Thirteen
Was God Racist?

Deuteronomy 14:2 *For thou art an holy people unto the LORD thy God, and the LORD hath chosen thee to be a peculiar people unto himself, above all the nations that are upon the earth.*

Let me read you a lengthy quote from an atheist website, complete with all of the spelling and grammatical errors:

"I would have thought the Bible of all books would be about love and peace for the whole world. I would never expected quotes from God or Jesus claiming only some ethnic groups were saved or that some were superior to others. But that is exactly what I found.

"First of all there is the constant claim that Jews are the 'chosen people'. Now surely a history of the Jews should teach a strong lesson of the dangers of declaring one group of people superior to all others. It always ends in trouble. Just ask the Germans.

"The Bible seems to have one rule for the Israelites and one rule for everyone else. If you don't see what's wrong with this remember that America had one-rule-for-us-another-rule-for-you laws. It was called Jim Crow.

"Before anyone says the Bible wasn't racist because he wasn't based on skin colour note that the United Nations defines racism as 'any distinction, exclusion, restriction or preference based on race, colour, descent, or national or ethnic origin'. So treating people different because they are from a different tribe or ethnic group is racist.

"In Deuteronomy chapter 7 the God tells the Israelites that there are other ethnic groups living in the promised land. Does God tell them to live in peace and harmony with them, with everyone respecting each others' differences? No he tells them 'to smite them, and utterly destroy them; thou shalt make no covenant with them nor shew mercy unto them. Neither shalt thou make marriages with them.' God commands the Israelites to exterminate another people, not for any crime but merely because they are a different ethnic group with a different religion. This exceeds even the Ku Klux Klan level of racism.

"Chapter 25 of the book of Numbers (verses 1-13) tells of when the Israelis began to inter-marry (it uses the term 'commit whoredom') with the Moabites, a neighbouring ethnic group with a different religion. This provoked the rage of God who commanded Moses to 'hang them'. One man had married a 'Midianitish'. An Israeli, Phinehas killed both of them with a javelin. God praises him for this and declares he 'hath turned my wrath away from the children of Israel.' He then rewards him with a 'covenant of peace' and the covenant of everlasting priesthood. Moral of the story, God doesn't want you to mix with people other you're own.

"Mixed marriages are denounced again. When Nehemiah was governor he found that Jews had inter-married with other ethnic groups. He 'cursed them, and smote certain of them' for committing 'this great evil'. He concludes with a malicious vague sentence Thus 'cleansed I them from all strangers'. (Nehemiah 13:23-30) The exact form of this ethnic cleansing is not described. Yet this is included (without criticism) in the Christian holy book and we are supposed to worship and live our lives according to it.

"Far from being open to all people, non-Israelis were actually banned from joining the religion. 'An Ammonite or Moabite shall not enter into the congregation of the LORD; even to their tenth generation shall they not enter into the congregation of the LORD for ever;' (Deuteronomy 23:3) So even if an extremely distant ancestor was from a neighbouring ethnic group, you could not become a Jew. Only pure Israelis could join.

"The book of Nehemiah (chapter 13) records that when people were told of this law, 'they separated from Israel all the mixed multitude.' (Nehemiah 13:3) So here we have an ancient version of ethnic cleansing."

(After a lengthy diatribe about Jesus, the author then concludes his screed this way:)

"For this reason, we should not try to base our lives or government on a book that you can use to justify literally any position. We should not pretend it is 'The Good Book'.

Morality and tolerance does not come from the Bible, it comes from society itself. We cannot worship nor blindly accept something that contains such blatantly racist comments. We should use our own ethics to judge the Bible not the other way around. Though, in doing so we are admitting that the Bible is redundant." (Nielsen)

It would be hard in anything other than a lengthy period of time to deal with all of the blatant errors of that lengthy quote. But we will deal with the most egregious ones, and then show the real truth about the God of the Old Testament and the supposed racism He demonstrated.

An evaluation of our supposedly moral and tolerant society

Let us begin where this internet skeptic ended:

"For this reason we should not try to base our lives or government on a book that you can use to justify literally any position. We should not pretend it is "The Good Book". **Morality and tolerance does not come from the Bible, it comes from society itself** (emphasis mine). We cannot worship nor blindly accept something that contains such blatantly racist comments. We should use our own ethics to judge the Bible not the other way around."

An old philosopher once said, "If one decided to turn away from Christ and the Bible, my question is, in the name of heaven, to what?"

That is an excellent question. Before we decide that the God of the Bible, or even just what the skeptic would call "The Old Testament God," is not worth following, we might want to make a comparison and see what other options there are. For the author of the above statement, the answer is "society." He says that morality and tolerance come from society.

The Soviet Union was an atheistic society, and they butchered tens of millions of their own people.

Cannibals have their society; tasty and deadly. Never eat at the Cannibal Café; their slogan is "Always Thinking of New Ways to Serve You."

Our society is no better. We have the highest violent crime and murder rate in the civilized world, and religion has nothing to do with it! It is not preachers and church members out there killing millions of people; it is gang bangers and druggies and thieves and thugs.

Turn on the news every night. You will not see people marching out of a church service looking for people to kill. You will see looting and rioting in "enlightened centers of society" because a jury verdict did not go someone's way or because a sports team won a game or because a sports team lost a game.

In 2013 there were 1,163,146 violent crimes reported to law enforcement, according to FBI records. Those million-plus crimes were not people running around "doing what God told them to do," they were not church sponsored witch hunts, they were our society doing what our society does.

There was a time when our society was nowhere near as violent. There was a time when people did not have to lock their doors, and no one had alarm systems.

Go back fifty years, you will not find metal detectors and automatic locking doors and security guards at schools.

Our country has tried as hard as it can to get rid of God and the Bible, and the result has been utterly predictable! Listen to this quote from Daniel Webster:

> "If religious books are not widely circulated among the masses in this country, I do not know what is going to become of us as a nation. If truth be not diffused, then error will be. If God and His Word are not known

and received, the devil and his works will gain the ascendency. If the evangelical volume does not reach every hamlet, the pages of a corrupt and licentious literature will. If the power of the gospel is not felt throughout the length and breadth of this land, **anarchy and misrule, degradation and misery, corruption and darkness** will reign without mitigation or end."

He nailed it. How many of you would drop your kids off down at some public playground and then leave them for a couple of hours while you run errands? None of you! And tell me: is it the Bible that you fear or society? Society.

It was not the Bible that beat me as a child and beat my mother in front of me. It was society, in the form of an abusive man.

It was not the Bible that twice grabbed gold chains from my jewelry store and ran; it was society, in the form of two criminals.

The subject matter at hand, by the way, is racism. And how well has "society" done with that? How about Saida Grundy, an "incoming Assistant Professor of Sociology and African-American Studies at Boston University?" In case that name does not ring a bell, this professor at a "tolerant, enlightened university" is openly racist against whites. She literally hates them and spews her hatred openly, and the university backs her up (Howell). So, tell me again, please, how we need to turn to our society for tolerance and morality since God is racist? By the way, I could give you thousands more examples just like her. Racism on university campuses is epidemic, especially against Jews.

Recently a young reporter named Ami Horowitz did an experiment. He went to the University of Berkeley, one of the most prestigious institutions on earth. He carried around an ISIS flag; you know, the people who are beheading Christians and raping children. He got cheered and high fived! Then he unfurled an Israeli flag and was booed and jeered. (Horowitz)

Society? No, society is not a good place to get our "morals and tolerance from." Not at all!

How many of you have had really, really bad experiences with society? And this is what this guy suggests we turn to for morality and tolerance! If you take every supposedly "mean racist" thing God ever did and put it into a pile, it would be a molehill compared to the Mount Everest size pile of racism and hatred and intolerance that society has produced without God!

And here is one more utterly hysterical thing to consider before we move on. Listen to this quote from the writer in question:

> "Before anyone says the Bible wasn't racist because he wasn't based on skin colour note that the United Nations defines racism as 'any distinction, exclusion, restriction or preference based on race, colour, descent, or national or ethnic origin.'"

Do you realize just how mind-boggling that quote is?

He is using the United Nations as his dictionary to define racism! There is quite literally no more corrupt, murderous, racist body of people on the entire planet than the United Nations! Listen to what Human Rights Watch executive director Kenneth Roth wrote in 2001:

> "Imagine a police force that includes murderers and rapists, or a police force run in large part by suspected murderers and rapists who are determined to stymie investigation of their crimes. Sadly, such spectacles are not far from reality at the United Nations Commission on Human Rights...
>
> "It features the sordid ritual of the world's despots and tyrants scrambling to join a commission that is tasked with investigating

183

and condemning the world's despots and tyrants...

"Dictatorships are as free as democracies to serve.

"The latest batch of new members illustrates how poorly the system works. They include such dubious paragons of human rights virtue as Algeria, the Democratic Republic of the Congo, Kenya, Libya, Saudia Arabia, Syria and Vietnam.

"Needless to say, such governments do not seek membership out of a commitment to promote human rights abroad or to improve their own abysmal human rights records. Rather they join the commission to protect themselves from criticism and to undermine its work." (Roth)

This is the UN, this is where this guy gets his authoritative definition of racism! This, by the way, is society at its finest: mass murderers being looked to as moral arbiters.

It would take someone blind and deaf, or just incredibly foolish, to actually look to society for morals and tolerance!

An examination of the supposed racism of God

The first thing the author of the hit piece on God took issue with, the first thing he used as "proof" of God's racism was that the Jews are referred to as God's "chosen people."

Let's do a little logic work, shall we?

Mr. So and So, is your wife your "chosen woman?" Since she is, that clearly means that you are "racist" toward every other woman, correct? Do you hate other women since you chose just that one?

That is utterly ridiculous. The fact that you have chosen one does not mean that you are racist or hateful toward anyone else. I love a lot of people, but I have one wife, and I love her *differently* than anyone else. If it is acceptable for us, why would it not be acceptable for God?

What about what the guy said:

> "Far from being open to all people, non-Israelis were actually banned from joining the religion. 'An Ammonite or Moabite shall not enter into the congregation of the LORD; even to their tenth generation shall they not enter into the congregation of the LORD for ever;' (Deuteronomy 23:3) So even if an extremely distant ancestor was from a neighbouring ethnic group, you could not become a Jew. Only pure Israelis could join."

You may want to know that there is not a period at the end of the verse this man quoted. In fact, though he puts a semicolon, there is actually supposed to be a colon. But regardless, the sentence does not end where he ends it. The reason he wants it to end there is because he wants you to believe that God was racist. But why don't we read all the way to the end of the sentence to see if race had anything at all to do with this:

Deuteronomy 23:3 *An Ammonite or Moabite shall not enter into the congregation of the LORD; even to their tenth generation shall they not enter into the congregation of the LORD for ever: 4 Because they met you not with bread and with water in the way, when ye came forth out of Egypt; and because they hired against thee Balaam the son of Beor of Pethor of Mesopotamia, to curse thee.*

God specifically stated why this prohibition was in place, and race had nothing to do with it. The Moabites and Ammonites tried to destroy Israel, so God put a ten-generation prohibition against them as punishment. That is very different from what this guy wants you to believe, now isn't it!

What about the prohibition against intermarriage? He mentions passages from Numbers and Nehemiah. In this case,

185

what is really interesting is the passage he conveniently left out. You see, there is actually one more passage in the Old Testament that strongly forbid the Jews from intermarrying. Why did he leave that one out? Because in that one, God actually told why they were not allowed to intermarry:

1 Kings 11:1 *But king Solomon loved many strange women, together with the daughter of Pharaoh, women of the Moabites, Ammonites, Edomites, Zidonians, and Hittites;* **2** *Of the nations concerning which the LORD said unto the children of Israel, Ye shall not go in to them, neither shall they come in unto you:* **for surely they will turn away your heart after their gods***: Solomon clave unto these in love.*

Now that is interesting, isn't it? The one passage he left out just so happens to be the one that explains that the prohibition against intermarriage did not have one thing to do with skin color or nationality; it was strictly about the fact that they would turn away the hearts of the people toward false gods, sending them to hell. It was not racism that prompted God to prohibit intermarriages; it was love! He did not want His people being condemned and separated from Him for eternity.

And that, friends, is why the God who is supposedly racist actually *allowed* certain intermarriages. Ruth was one of those Moabites that they were forbidden to marry, yet God brought her right to Boaz to marry. Why? Because she had already given her heart to the God of Israel! Rahab was one of those Canaanites that they were forbidden to marry, yet God brought her right to Salmon to marry. Why? Because she had already given her heart to the God of Israel! And are you ready for this? Not only were those two women of different races allowed to marry into Israel, they were allowed to marry into the choicest part; both of them ended up in the bloodline of Christ, the Son of God!

I can just imagine Jesus, in heaven, hearing Himself described as a racist, and saying "Hey, great gramma Rahab, great gramma Ruth, do you hear what that guy just said?"

Here is one last quote:

"In Deuteronomy chapter 7 the God tells the Israelites that there are other ethnic groups living in the promised land. Does God tell them to live in peace and harmony with them, with everyone respecting each others' differences? No he tells them 'to smite them, and utterly destroy them; thou shalt make no covenant with them nor shew mercy unto them. Neither shalt thou make marriages with them.' God commands the Israelites to exterminate another people, not for any crime but merely because they are a different ethnic group with a different religion. This exceeds even the Ku Klux Klan level of racism."

How about that? God tells His people to swoop in and wipe people out just because of their religion, rather than living with them in peace and harmony!

Let me, first of all, ask you a question: when has there ever, EVER been peace and harmony in the Middle East? The notion that Israel would be allowed to live there in "peace and harmony" is a bigger fairy tale than Peter Pan. In fact, look at this:

Exodus 17:8 *Then came Amalek, and fought with Israel in Rephidim.*

Please notice that this is well before the passage this man quotes from Deuteronomy. Before Israel even got near to the Promised Land, people from the Promised Land were coming out to meet them in the wilderness to try and destroy them! If this guy actually thinks Israel would ever be allowed to live in peace and harmony, if he thinks the Canaanites were just going to "make room for their new neighbors," then he is utterly foolish.

This land had already been the land of Abraham and his descendants, given to them by God. While they were gone for four hundred years as slaves in Egypt, others filled it up.

187

When they came back home, they were going to have to fight for it and race had nothing to do with it.

By the way, this is pointed to as an example of God's supposed racism, but here is a verse that will show you something very different, God's patience:

Genesis 15:12 *And when the sun was going down, a deep sleep fell upon Abram; and, lo, an horror of great darkness fell upon him.* **13** *And he said unto Abram, Know of a surety that thy seed shall be a stranger in a land that is not theirs, and shall serve them; and they shall afflict them four hundred years;* **14** *And also that nation, whom they shall serve, will I judge: and afterward shall they come out with great substance.* **15** *And thou shalt go to thy fathers in peace; thou shalt be buried in a good old age.* **16** *But in the fourth generation they shall come hither again:* ***for the iniquity of the Amorites is not yet full.***

In the days of Abraham, the Amorites were already incredibly wicked. Yet God told Abraham that it would be four hundred years before He would deal with them. He was patient with them until they were so incredibly wicked and unrepentant that God removed them. That is incredibly patient.

The Old Testament is filled with examples of God being incredibly kind to people who came to Him regardless of race. Yes, Israel was His chosen people, but no, that does not make Him a racist at all, skin had nothing to do with any prohibitions He put into place.

An explanation of why God placed the Jews on a special plane

To this day, Israel is God's chosen people as far as *nationalities* go. But why would God put any nation on that special plane? Why not put every nation on the same plane?

There are two answers to that question, one deals with origins, the other with conclusions.

On the origins side, God put Israel on a special plane because one man chose to be different than all of the rest of the world. His name was Abraham:

James 2:23 *And the scripture was fulfilled which saith, Abraham believed God, and it was imputed unto him for righteousness: and he was called the Friend of God.*

In a time when the world was wicked and sensual and polytheistic, one man walked with God. Because of Abraham's love for God when no one else cared, God made him a promise:

Genesis 12:1 *Now the LORD had said unto Abram, Get thee out of thy country, and from thy kindred, and from thy father's house, unto a land that I will shew thee:* **2** *And I will make of thee a great nation, and I will bless thee, and make thy name great; and thou shalt be a blessing:* **3** *And I will bless them that bless thee, and curse him that curseth thee: and in thee shall all families of the earth be blessed.*

Abraham is mentioned hundreds of times in the Bible, both Old and New Testament. His faith and obedience resulted in God promising to love and protect his descendants.

Anyone else on earth could have done what Abraham did, but none did, just him.

On the conclusion side, let us go to the New Testament:

Romans 3:1 *What advantage then hath the Jew? or what profit is there of circumcision?* **2** *Much every way: chiefly, because that unto them were committed the oracles of God.*

Hebrews 7:14 *For it is evident that our Lord sprang out of Juda; of which tribe Moses spake nothing concerning priesthood.*

These two verses teach us something. There were two very special things God desired to give the world; His Son, and the Bible. He needed a people to do that through. He gave us both His Son and the Bible through the Jewish people. The fact that He chose them has not been a bad thing for us, it has been the best thing ever for us because they gave us our Savior and our Bible!

God was not, is not, never has been a racist.

Chapter Fourteen
The Breach of Uzzah

2 Samuel 6:1 *Again, David gathered together all the chosen men of Israel, thirty thousand.* **2** *And David arose, and went with all the people that were with him from Baale of Judah, to bring up from thence the ark of God, whose name is called by the name of the LORD of hosts that dwelleth between the cherubims.* **3** *And they set the ark of God upon a new cart, and brought it out of the house of Abinadab that was in Gibeah: and Uzzah and Ahio, the sons of Abinadab, drave the new cart.* **4** *And they brought it out of the house of Abinadab which was at Gibeah, accompanying the ark of God: and Ahio went before the ark.* **5** *And David and all the house of Israel played before the LORD on all manner of instruments made of fir wood, even on harps, and on psalteries, and on timbrels, and on cornets, and on cymbals.* **6** *And when they came to Nachon's threshingfloor, Uzzah put forth his hand to the ark of God, and took hold of it; for the oxen shook it.* **7** *And the anger of the LORD was kindled against Uzzah; and God smote him there for his error; and there he died by the ark of God.* **8** *And David was displeased, because the LORD had made a breach upon Uzzah: and he called the name of the place Perezuzzah to this day.* **9** *And David was afraid of the LORD that day, and said, How shall the ark of the LORD come to me?* **10** *So David would not remove the ark of the LORD unto him into the city of David:*

but David carried it aside into the house of Obededom the Gittite.

I put out a note online recently asking people to tell me what things they saw in the Old Testament that made them feel like God was unjust even though they knew He wasn't. It was not a surprise to me when this came up. I remember reading this as a little boy and thinking, "Man, that is harsh!"

It is my desire through this entire book to peel back the layers of each thing we see like that and reveal God for what He really is. Not harsh, but holy. But also, let us never forget, compassionate and loving, so much so that He sent His Son to die for us. So, let us study our way through "The Breach of Uzzah."

The background of the Ark

When Israel was freed from Egypt hundreds of years earlier by God through Moses, God took them out into the wilderness and taught them how He expected to be worshiped. One of the vital parts of that worship was a special piece of furniture called the Ark of the Covenant, or the Ark of God. It was a wooden box covered in gold, with a couple of golden angels mounted on top of it. While it was in the wilderness tabernacle, the very presence of God would rest on it. It was literally the spot where God would meet with His people.

Exodus 25:9 *According to all that I shew thee, after the pattern of the tabernacle, and the pattern of all the instruments thereof, even so shall ye make it.* **10** *And they shall make an ark of shittim wood: two cubits and a half shall be the length thereof, and a cubit and a half the breadth thereof, and a cubit and a half the height thereof.* **11** *And thou shalt overlay it with pure gold, within and without shalt thou overlay it, and shalt make upon it a crown of gold round about.* **12** *And thou shalt cast four rings of gold for it, and put them in the four corners thereof; and two rings shall be in the* one side of it, and two rings in the other side of it. **13** *And thou shalt make staves of shittim wood, and overlay them with gold.* **14** *And thou shalt put the staves into the rings by the sides of the ark, that the ark may be borne with them.* **15** *The staves shall be in the rings of the ark: they shall not be taken from it.* **16** *And thou shalt put into the ark the testimony which I shall give thee.* **17** *And thou shalt make a mercy seat of pure gold: two cubits and a half shall be the length thereof, and a cubit and a half the breadth thereof.* **18** *And thou shalt make two cherubims of gold, of beaten work shalt thou make them, in the two ends of the mercy seat.* **19** *And make one cherub on the one end, and the other cherub on the other end: even of the mercy seat shall ye make the cherubims on the two ends thereof.* **20** *And the cherubims shall stretch forth their wings on high, covering the mercy seat with their wings, and their faces shall look one to another; toward the mercy seat shall the faces of the cherubims be.* **21** *And thou shalt put the mercy seat above upon the ark; and in the ark thou shalt put the testimony that I shall give thee.* **22** ***And there I will meet with thee, and I will commune with thee from above the mercy seat****, from between the two cherubims which are upon the ark of the testimony, of all things which I will give thee in commandment unto the children of Israel.*

Exodus 30:6 *And thou shalt put it before the vail that is by the ark of the testimony, before the mercy seat that is over the testimony,* ***where I will meet with thee****.*

This was such a sacred object, that not only could no one touch it, no one was even allowed to come near it except for the high priest, and he could only come near at certain appointed times:

Leviticus 16:1 *And the LORD spake unto Moses after the death of the two sons of Aaron, when they offered before the LORD, and died;* **2** *And the LORD said unto Moses, Speak unto Aaron thy brother, that he come not at all times into the holy place within the vail before the mercy seat,*

which is upon the ark; that he die not: for I will appear in the
cloud upon the mercy seat.

Adam Clarke said of this verse:

"In ordinary cases the high priest could enter this place only once in the year, that is, on the day of annual atonement; but in extraordinary cases he might enter more frequently, viz., while in the wilderness, in decamping and encamping, he must enter to take down or adjust the things; and on solemn pressing public occasions, he was obliged to enter in order to consult the Lord: but he never entered without the deepest reverence and due preparation." (1:561)

This piece of furniture was the absolute heart of the nation of Israel. If you were to wrap the Constitution and the Declaration of Independence and the flag that flew over Fort McHenry and the remains of the Unknown Soldier up in one box, that would not even begin to come close to how important the Ark of the Covenant was to Israel.

The beginning of a disaster

As important as the Ark was, you would think that the Children of Israel would never ever take it lightly. But Israel never seemed to rise above the level of her leaders, and she did not always have good leaders. One of those very bad ones was a high priest named Eli. His sin was that he allowed his sons into the priesthood and did not remove them even when they committed the most vile of sins:

1 Samuel 2:12 *Now the sons of Eli were sons of Belial; they knew not the LORD.* **13** *And the priests' custom with the people was, that, when any man offered sacrifice, the priest's servant came, while the flesh was in seething, with a fleshhook of three teeth in his hand;* **14** *And he struck it into the pan, or kettle, or caldron, or pot; all that the fleshhook brought up the priest took for himself. So they did in Shiloh*

194

unto all the Israelites that came thither. **15** *Also before they burnt the fat, the priest's servant came, and said to the man that sacrificed, Give flesh to roast for the priest; for he will not have sodden flesh of thee, but raw.* **16** *And if any man said unto him, Let them not fail to burn the fat presently, and then take as much as thy soul desireth; then he would answer him, Nay; but thou shalt give it me now: and if not, I will take it by force.* **17** *Wherefore the sin of the young men was very great before the LORD: for men abhorred the offering of the LORD.*

Now skip down to verse twenty-two:

1 Samuel 2:22 *Now Eli was very old, and heard all that his sons did unto all Israel; and how they lay with the women that assembled at the door of the tabernacle of the congregation.* **23** *And he said unto them, Why do ye such things? for I hear of your evil dealings by all this people.* **24** *Nay, my sons; for it is no good report that I hear: ye make the LORD'S people to transgress.* **25** *If one man sin against another, the judge shall judge him: but if a man sin against the LORD, who shall intreat for him? Notwithstanding they hearkened not unto the voice of their father, because the LORD would slay them.*

Notice that Eli *spoke* to them about their wrong, but that is all he did. Now look at this:

1 Samuel 3:11 *And the LORD said to Samuel, Behold, I will do a thing in Israel, at which both the ears of every one that heareth it shall tingle.* **12** *In that day I will perform against Eli all things which I have spoken concerning his house: when I begin, I will also make an end.* **13** *For I have told him that I will judge his house for ever for the iniquity which he knoweth; because his sons made themselves vile, and **he restrained them not**.*

That was the condition of the leadership in Israel at the time. And because of that, Israel was just as bad, just as unspiritual. And that is why you see the calamity that happened next:

195

1 Samuel 4:2 *And the Philistines put themselves in array against Israel: and when they joined battle, Israel was smitten before the Philistines: and they slew of the army in the field about four thousand men. 3 And when the people were come into the camp, the elders of Israel said, Wherefore hath the LORD smitten us to day before the Philistines? Let us fetch the ark of the covenant of the LORD out of Shiloh unto us, that, when it cometh among us, it may save us out of the hand of our enemies. 4 So the people sent to Shiloh, that they might bring from thence the ark of the covenant of the LORD of hosts, which dwelleth between the cherubims: and the two sons of Eli, Hophni and Phinehas, were there with the ark of the covenant of God. 5 And when the ark of the covenant of the LORD came into the camp, all Israel shouted with a great shout, so that the earth rang again. 6 And when the Philistines heard the noise of the shout, they said, What meaneth the noise of this great shout in the camp of the Hebrews? And they understood that the ark of the LORD was come into the camp. 7 And the Philistines were afraid, for they said, God is come into the camp. And they said, Woe unto us! for there hath not been such a thing heretofore. 8 Woe unto us! who shall deliver us out of the hand of these mighty Gods? these are the Gods that smote the Egyptians with all the plagues in the wilderness. 9 Be strong, and quit yourselves like men, O ye Philistines, that ye be not servants unto the Hebrews, as they have been to you: quit yourselves like men, and fight. 10 And the Philistines fought, and Israel was smitten, and they fled every man into his tent: and there was a very great slaughter; for there fell of Israel thirty thousand footmen. 11 **And the ark of God was taken**; and the two sons of Eli, Hophni and Phinehas, were slain.*

The Ark of God was nothing more than a magic box to Israel at that point in time. It had been reduced to the level of a good luck charm in their thinking. God would have none of that, so He allowed it to be taken in battle.

The Philistines did not know what to do or not do with it, and God ended up killing a great number of them. So, after seven months they loaded it up onto a cart and shipped it back to the Israelites!

It is then that something unimaginable happened. The children of Israel basically forgot that it even existed.

In 1 Samuel 7, we find that it ended up in the house of a man named Abinadab. This thing which should have been the centerpiece of the entire nation became a dust collector in the house of one man. Verse two tells us that it was there for twenty years before anyone even began to mourn for it and for God. After that period of twenty years, we come to 1 Samuel 8-9, where the people demanded and received a king. That king's name was Saul, and according to Acts 13:21 he ruled for 40 years. All that time, the ark was still in the house of Abinadab. Finally, after Saul, David became king. Somewhere in the early years of the reign of David, we come to 2 Samuel 6, and we find David finally bringing the Ark back out into the nation again and setting up a house for it. In other words, it had been gone for at the very least sixty years. Sixty years! The most important object in Jewish life had been gone since before David was born!

The breach of Uzzah

Everything that we have just seen will play a critical role in what we see happen to Uzzah.

After having been gone and forgotten for at least sixty years, King David began to think back on the history of His people, and he remembered the tales of the Ark of God.

2 Samuel 6:1 *Again, David gathered together all the chosen men of Israel, thirty thousand.* **2** *And David arose, and went with all the people that were with him from Baale of Judah, to bring up from thence the ark of God, whose name is called by the name of the LORD of hosts that dwelleth between the cherubims.*

One thing we need to clearly establish is that, for a change, the motive of everyone involved was right.

David was right to want to bring the Ark of God and the presence of God back into the center of the nation's life.

Uzzah was also right to want to make sure it did not fall off of the cart:

2 Samuel 6:6 *And when they came to Nachon's threshingfloor, Uzzah put forth his hand to the ark of God, and took hold of it; for the oxen shook it.*

This was not some inquisitive Philistine trying to find out what was inside the box.

This was not some arrogant son of a priest who did not care about the Ark or the God of the Ark.

Uzzah just wanted to keep it from falling; his motives were pure. And the fact that everyone's motives were pure and right is what can make us do as I did as a child, shaking my head and saying, "Man, that is harsh!"

But once again, God is not harsh; He is holy. But He is also loving and compassionate.

That said, Uzzah did die because of some things that were done wrong. Three of them in fact, three very important ones. Two of those wrongdoings were his, but one was David's.

David's wrong was something that he himself later lets us in on. We find this in a parallel account of the breach of Uzzah.

1 Chronicles 15:1 *And David made him houses in the city of David, and prepared a place for the ark of God, and pitched for it a tent. 2 Then David said, None ought to carry the ark of God but the Levites: for them hath the LORD chosen to carry the ark of God, and to minister unto him for ever. 3 And David gathered all Israel together to Jerusalem, to bring up the ark of the LORD unto his place, which he had prepared for it. 4 And David assembled the children of Aaron, and the Levites: 5 Of the sons of Kohath; Uriel the chief, and his brethren an hundred and twenty: 6 Of the sons* of Merari; Asaiah the chief, and his brethren two hundred and twenty: **7** Of the sons of Gershom; Joel the chief, and his brethren an hundred and thirty: **8** Of the sons of Elizaphan; Shemaiah the chief, and his brethren two hundred: **9** Of the sons of Hebron; Eliel the chief, and his brethren fourscore: **10** Of the sons of Uzziel; Amminadab the chief, and his brethren an hundred and twelve. **11** And David called for Zadok and Abiathar the priests, and for the Levites, for Uriel, Asaiah, and Joel, Shemaiah, and Eliel, and Amminadab, **12** And said unto them, Ye are the chief of the fathers of the Levites: sanctify yourselves, both ye and your brethren, that ye may bring up the ark of the LORD God of Israel unto the place that I have prepared for it. **13 For because ye did it not at the first, the LORD our God made a breach upon us, for that we sought him not after the due order. 14** So the priests and the Levites sanctified themselves to bring up the ark of the LORD God of Israel. **15 And the children of the Levites bare the ark of God upon their shoulders with the staves thereon, as Moses commanded according to the word of the LORD.**

There were only a handful of people that were allowed to carry the Ark, and there was a specific way it had to be done. David's sin, according to his own words in verse thirteen, was "not seeking God after the due order."

In other words, God had already given them very specific instructions as to how to handle all of this, and David did not bother to read those instructions.

Who exactly was responsible for making sure that no one died in bringing the Ark back? King David. All he had to do was read the instructions given to Moses, and Uzzah never would have died. The foreman in charge of the job did not do his job, and one of the workers died as a result.

Think of it in terms of a huge electrical job. Electricity can kill. On a huge electrical job, that foreman has to make everyone aware of the danger, and he has to make sure that everyone knows what to do and what not to do. Electricity does what it does. If it is handled right, it brings power. If it is handled wrong, it brings injury or death. Uzzah died because David did not take things seriously enough to read the instructions and make sure everyone followed them:

Exodus 25:14 *And thou shalt put the staves into the rings by the sides of the ark, that the ark may be borne with them.* **15** *The staves shall be in the rings of the ark: they shall not be taken from it.*

Those rings and staves were like a giant "Do not touch!" sign.

But there are two other sins that led to Uzzah's death. The first one is painfully obvious: he touched the Ark. It simply was not allowed. This was not like anything else in Jewish life. There was no excuse for anyone at all to ever touch it.

But there was a third sin involved, one that to me is the most profound of all. Look carefully at something we skimmed over just a bit ago:

1 Samuel 7:1 *And the men of Kirjathjearim came, and fetched up the ark of the LORD, and brought it into the house of Abinadab in the hill, and sanctified Eleazar his son to keep the ark of the LORD.*

When the ark of God came back from Philistine territory, it was placed into the house of Abinadab. His son Eleazar was sanctified to be its caretaker.

Now fast forward sixty years or so:

2 Samuel 6:3 *And they set the ark of God upon a new cart, and brought it out of the house of Abinadab that was in Gibeah: and* **Uzzah and Ahio, the sons of Abinadab,** *drave the new cart.*

When we think of Uzzah being killed for reaching out and touching the Ark, we need to realize that we are not dealing with someone who had never been around the Ark. In fact, we are dealing with someone who *had never not been around the Ark!*

This man had literally grown up with it in his house. His brother was its caretaker. It is evident that he had never touched it before, or he would not be alive at this point to be driving the cart. In other words, he had grown up being told "Don't touch that! Don't touch that! That is the Ark of God, it is special!"

But do you know what happened somewhere along the way? Somewhere along the way, Uzzah got way too familiar with the Ark of God. Because he was around it all the time, he dropped his guard; he got comfortable around it.

When God killed Uzzah for touching the Ark, He killed one of the two or three people in the land that really ought to have known better. Very few people in the entire nation had ever even seen the Ark! If someone else reached out and touched it, it would have been much easier to understand their error. But how exactly does a man who has grown up hearing "Don't touch that!" reach out and touch it?

I am not at all denigrating the motive of Uzzah. To me it is very clear that his heart was in the right place; he just did not want it to fall. But if anyone knew better, Uzzah knew better. If Bobby or Susie or Tom or Sally had reached out and touched it, they may just not have known better. But Uzzah? Uzzah of all people knew not to touch it. The problem was, he had gotten familiar with God, *and lost his reverence*.

There is an incredible spiritual lesson to be learned from the death of Uzzah. We have all grown up in America around the preaching and the presence of God. But we would do well not to get so familiar *with Him* that we lose our reverence *for Him.*

Chapter Fifteen
When David Numbered the People

2 Samuel 24:1 *And again the anger of the LORD was kindled against Israel, and he moved David against them to say, Go, number Israel and Judah.* **2** *For the king said to Joab the captain of the host, which was with him, Go now through all the tribes of Israel, from Dan even to Beersheba, and number ye the people, that I may know the number of the people.* **3** *And Joab said unto the king, Now the LORD thy God add unto the people, how many soever they be, an hundredfold, and that the eyes of my lord the king may see it: but why doth my lord the king delight in this thing?* **4** *Notwithstanding the king's word prevailed against Joab, and against the captains of the host. And Joab and the captains of the host went out from the presence of the king, to number the people of Israel.* **5** *And they passed over Jordan, and pitched in Aroer, on the right side of the city that lieth in the midst of the river of Gad, and toward Jazer:* **6** *Then they came to Gilead, and to the land of Tahtimhodshi; and they came to Danjaan, and about to Zidon,* **7** *And came to the strong hold of Tyre, and to all the cities of the Hivites, and of the Canaanites: and they went out to the south of Judah, even to Beersheba.* **8** *So when they had gone through all the land, they came to Jerusalem at the end of nine months and twenty days.* **9** *And Joab gave up the sum of the number of the people unto the king: and there were in Israel eight hundred* thousand valiant men that drew the sword; and the men of Judah were five hundred thousand men. **10** And David's heart smote him after that he had numbered the people. And David said unto the LORD, I have sinned greatly in that I have done: and now, I beseech thee, O LORD, take away the iniquity of thy servant; for I have done very foolishly. **11** For when David was up in the morning, the word of the LORD came unto the prophet Gad, David's seer, saying, **12** Go and say unto David, Thus saith the LORD, I offer thee three things; choose thee one of them, that I may do it unto thee. **13** So Gad came to David, and told him, and said unto him, Shall seven years of famine come unto thee in thy land? or wilt thou flee three months before thine enemies, while they pursue thee? or that there be three days' pestilence in thy land? now advise, and see what answer I shall return to him that sent me. **14** And David said unto Gad, I am in a great strait: let us fall now into the hand of the LORD; for his mercies are great: and let me not fall into the hand of man. **15** So the LORD sent a pestilence upon Israel from the morning even to the time appointed: and there died of the people from Dan even to Beersheba seventy thousand men. **16** And when the angel stretched out his hand upon Jerusalem to destroy it, the LORD repented him of the evil, and said to the angel that destroyed the people, It is enough: stay now thine hand. And the angel of the LORD was by the threshingplace of Araunah the Jebusite. **17** And David spake unto the LORD when he saw the angel that smote the people, and said, Lo, I have sinned, and I have done wickedly: but these sheep, what have they done? let thine hand, I pray thee, be against me, and against my father's house.

1 Chronicles 21:1 And Satan stood up against Israel, and provoked David to number Israel. **2** And David said to Joab and to the rulers of the people, Go, number Israel from Beersheba even to Dan; and bring the number of them to me, that I may know it. **3** And Joab answered, The LORD make his people an hundred times so many more as they be: but, my lord the king, are they not all my lord's servants? why then doth my lord require this thing? why will he be a cause of trespass to Israel? **4** Nevertheless the king's word prevailed against Joab. Wherefore Joab departed, and went throughout all Israel, and came to Jerusalem. **5** And Joab gave the sum of the number of the people unto David. And all they of Israel were a thousand thousand and an hundred thousand men that drew sword: and Judah was four hundred threescore and ten thousand men that drew sword. **6** But Levi and Benjamin counted he not among them: for the king's word was abominable to Joab. **7** And God was displeased with this thing; therefore he smote Israel. **8** And David said unto God, I have sinned greatly, because I have done this thing: but now, I beseech thee, do away the iniquity of thy servant; for I have done very foolishly. **9** And the LORD spake unto Gad, David's seer, saying, **10** Go and tell David, saying, Thus saith the LORD, I offer thee three things: choose thee one of them, that I may do it unto thee. **11** So Gad came to David, and said unto him, Thus saith the LORD, Choose thee **12** Either three years' famine; or three months to be destroyed before thy foes, while that the sword of thine enemies overtaketh thee; or else three days the sword of the LORD, even the pestilence, in the land, and the angel of the LORD destroying throughout all the coasts of Israel. Now therefore advise thyself what word I shall bring again to him that sent me. **13** And David said unto Gad, I am in a great strait: let me fall now into the hand of the LORD; for very great are his mercies: but let me not fall into the hand of man. **14** So the LORD sent pestilence upon Israel: and there fell of Israel seventy thousand men. **15** And God sent an angel unto Jerusalem to destroy it: and as he was destroying, the LORD beheld, and he repented him of the evil, and said to the angel that destroyed, It is enough, stay now thine hand. And the angel of the LORD stood by the threshingfloor of Ornan the Jebusite. **16** And David lifted up his eyes, and saw the angel of the LORD stand between the earth and the heaven, having

205

a drawn sword in his hand stretched out over Jerusalem. Then David and the elders of Israel, who were clothed in sackcloth, fell upon their faces. **17** *And David said unto God, Is it not I that commanded the people to be numbered? even I it is that have sinned and done evil indeed; but as for these sheep, what have they done? let thine hand, I pray thee, O LORD my God, be on me, and on my father's house; but not on thy people, that they should be plagued.*

The two passages we have read are parallel accounts of the same event. It is an episode that has caused many a shaken head and raised eyebrow through the years. In a nutshell, David sinned, and a great many other people died because of what he had done.

This certainly needs to be examined and deciphered, lest we come to wrong conclusions about God. So, let's dig in.

The oddity of the sin

There are certain sins in Scripture that we see, and our immediate reaction is, "Yep, that was bad; he is in for it!" And then, on the far other end of the spectrum, there is this.

As we read this, on the surface it is very hard to see what the big deal is. I say that simply because there are so many other instances in the Bible where a king or ruler numbered the people, and it was not regarded as a sin. For instance:

Numbers 1:1 *And the LORD spake unto Moses in the wilderness of Sinai, in the tabernacle of the congregation, on the first day of the second month, in the second year after they were come out of the land of Egypt, saying,* **2** *Take ye the sum of all the congregation of the children of Israel, after their families, by the house of their fathers, with the number of their names, every male by their polls;* **3** *From twenty years old and upward, all that are able to go forth to war in Israel: thou and Aaron shall number them by their armies.*

206

Joshua 8:10 *And Joshua rose up early in the morning, and numbered the people, and went up, he and the elders of Israel, before the people to Ai.*

Judges 21:9 *For the people were numbered, and, behold, there were none of the inhabitants of Jabeshgilead there.*

1 Samuel 13:15 *And Samuel arose, and gat him up from Gilgal unto Gibeah of Benjamin. And Saul numbered the people that were present with him, about six hundred men.*

1 Samuel 15:4 *And Saul gathered the people together, and numbered them in Telaim, two hundred thousand footmen, and ten thousand men of Judah.*

In all of those cases, someone numbered the people, and it was not regarded as a sin. That makes what we see in our text seem like such an oddity. Why, in that particular case, was it regarded as being such an incredibly huge sin?

This is clearly something that we can learn from.

What facts do we have to work with?

One: At other times, numbering the people was not a sin.

Two: At this time, numbering the people was a sin.

Three: No one was caught off guard by the fact that this was a sin at this time. Even someone as spiritually bankrupt as Joab knew it! Look at this:

1 Chronicles 21:3 *And Joab answered, The LORD make his people an hundred times so many more as they be: but, my lord the king, are they not all my lord's servants? why then doth my lord require this thing? why will he be a cause of trespass to Israel? 4 Nevertheless the king's word prevailed against Joab. Wherefore Joab departed, and went throughout all Israel, and came to Jerusalem. 5 And Joab gave the sum of the number of the people unto David. And all they of Israel were a thousand thousand and an hundred thousand men that drew sword: and Judah was four hundred threescore and ten thousand men that drew sword. 6 But Levi* *and Benjamin counted he not among them: for the king's word was abominable to Joab.*

When you study the life of Joab, you will find him to be among the most wicked of sinners. He was a murderer, a liar, and quite likely a blackmailer.

He murdered the king's own son while he was hanging in a tree utterly defenseless.

When someone *that* evil looks at what you are about to do and thinks that it is awful, trust me, what you are doing is utterly awful! This would be like Bill Clinton being truly embarrassed over your level of dishonesty!

"I mean, yeah, I told a lie about Monica, but good night, man, are you really gonna tell a whopper that big? You ought not to do that; that's terrible!"

What David was doing, he knew to be a sin. Joab knew it to be a sin. Everybody knew it to be a sin.

Most people speculate that this was a sin of pride; that David was only numbering the people to stoke his own ego. That may well be correct. But the real thing you need to see from this is that *things that are right at one point can be wrong at another point if God for some reason has said "no" at that point!*

Let me say that again: *"Things that are right at one point can be wrong at another point if God for some reason has said 'no' at that point!"*

There are multiple ways that something can be wrong, and they are as follows: what you do, why you do it, who does it or to whom it is done, where it is done, or when it is done.

You can easily think through Scripture of people who did wrong in each of the above ways. Cain did a "what" wrong when he killed Abel. James spoke of people doing a "why" wrong when he mentioned people praying specifically so that they could have something to fulfill their lust. David and Bathsheba committed the "who" and "whom" wrong in their adultery. The Corinthians did a "where" wrong by having their elaborate feasts in front of poor people in the church at the Lord's supper instead of at home.

And in the case, we see in our text, David committed a "when" wrong by numbering the people at a time when God clearly did not want it to be done.

In everything we do, we need to be very careful to seek the **current** will of God. There have been things I prayed about for years, and God said "no, no, no" and then one day the no changed to a yes.

There have been things we have done in God's perfect will for years, and then one day God clearly said "no more.' For us to do the next day the same thing that we rightly did the previous day would have actually been wrong the next day.

The list of "right and wrongs" of Scripture does not just include actions that are always either/or. A right or a wrong can also be determined by God's will at that present moment. He has His reasons, and we need to pay attention.

Each day my son asks for my phone to play a particular game for a few minutes. On most days I say yes. On some days I say no. If he does it on the day I say yes, he has not done wrong. If he does that exact same thing on a day I say no, he has done wrong. For whatever the reason, God did not want David to number the people at that time, and David did it anyway. He knew it was wrong; wicked old Joab knew it was wrong; everybody knew it was wrong.

The origin of the temptation

All throughout the first point, I emphasized that God did not want the numbering done at that particular time. And I am quite certain that as I did, many of your minds were going right back to the very first verse we read:

2 Samuel 24:1 *And again the anger of the LORD was kindled against Israel, and he moved David against them to say, Go, number Israel and Judah.*

Others of you were not only thinking of that verse, but you were also racing ahead in your mind to what critics often point to as a supposed contradiction in Scripture:

1 Chronicles 21:1 *And Satan stood up against Israel, and provoked David to number Israel.*

What have we here? Did God originate the temptation for David to sin? Did the devil do it? This is incredibly essential; we need to know!

The first thing we should clearly establish is that, just on a logical level alone, there is not a contradiction here. Please allow me to illustrate that. You have two children, and they do not like your Chihuahua. The girl builds a rocket out of household appliances, with the idea of sending the dog into outer space. The boy straps the Chihuahua to the rocket and lights the fuse. Who is responsible for the fact that the Chihuahua is now orbiting the earth?

Both of them. If the mom says, "The boy did it!" and the dad says, "The girl did it!" they are not saying things that are contradictory; they are saying things that are complimentary. When you read these two passages and want to know which one is in error, the answer is "neither." When you read these two passages and want to know which one is correct, the answer is "both."

1 Samuel tells us of God's involvement while 1 Chronicles tells us of the devil's involvement; both passages are correct.

The question then becomes whether or not a word study can decipher the seeming mystery for us. The answer to that is "yes and no." Samuel tells us that God "moved" David to do this, Chronicles tells us that Satan "provoked" David to do it. Both of these words are actually from the identical Hebrew word, the word *cuwth*. But if they are from the same word, why are they translated two different ways?

As we point out so often, in every single language on earth words have multiple meanings. Gay can mean "happy," or it can mean "homosexual." Pull can mean actually pulling something toward you, or it can mean "influence."

The Hebrew word used in these two accounts also has multiple meanings. One of them is "to instigate." Another is simply "to move."

When you read these two passages, you will note that our translators used the word "provoked," but only once, and only in reference to what the devil did. When it came to what God did, they used the word "moved." One is a term of origination, the other in this instance is a term of continuation. In other words, the devil started the process in David's heart, and when he responded to it, God continued it by giving him a push.

We find the exact same thing in reference to God's dealings with Pharaoh. We read beginning in Exodus 7 that God hardened Pharaoh's heart, but when we go backwards to chapter five, we find that Pharaoh himself began the process by rejecting Moses and the God of Moses.

The originator of the sin of David was the devil, the one who chose to act on that origination was David, and the one who moved the process along after that was God.

Another way to put it is that the devil tempted, David agreed, and God in so many words said, "If that is the way you want to go, I will grease the skids for you."

The overthrow of the "innocent"

2 Samuel 24:11 *For when David was up in the morning, the word of the LORD came unto the prophet Gad, David's seer, saying,* **12** *Go and say unto David, Thus saith the LORD, I offer thee three things; choose thee one of them, that I may do it unto thee.* **13** *So Gad came to David, and told him, and said unto him, Shall seven years of famine come unto thee in thy land? or wilt thou flee three months before thine enemies, while they pursue thee? or that there be three days' pestilence in thy land? now advise, and see what answer I shall return to him that sent me.* **14** *And David said*

211

unto Gad, I am in a great strait: let us fall now into the hand of the LORD; for his mercies are great: and let me not fall into the hand of man. **15** *So the LORD sent a pestilence upon Israel from the morning even to the time appointed: and there died of the people from Dan even to Beersheba seventy thousand men.* **16** *And when the angel stretched out his hand upon Jerusalem to destroy it, the LORD repented him of the evil, and said to the angel that destroyed the people, It is enough: stay now thine hand. And the angel of the LORD was by the threshingplace of Araunah the Jebusite.* **17** *And David spake unto the LORD when he saw the angel that smote the people, and said, Lo, I have sinned, and I have done wickedly: but these sheep, what have they done? let thine hand, I pray thee, be against me, and against my father's house.*

When we look at the judgment that fell on the people over David's sin, we can easily see how the character of God can come under attack. Seventy thousand people died, and yet David lived! Even David himself seems to question God's character, asking why these "sheep" should suffer for what he had done.

We will deal with one part of that now and then cover it from another angle in our final point. The part I want to deal with right now is the question of whose sin really caused all of this? The answer is obvious but usually missed. And the reason it is usually missed is because people get emotional over a perceived injustice, and emotion makes a very poor investigative tool. So just for a moment let us become very dispassionate and take a look back at the very beginning of all of this.

2 Samuel 24:1 *And again the anger of the LORD was kindled against Israel, and he moved David against them to say, Go, number Israel and Judah.*

Who was God angry with? This verse clearly tells us that His anger was directed at Israel, the nation, the people. We are nowhere told what their sin was, but whatever it was, it was bad enough for the devil to see an opening, a chance that he may be able to use it to get God to judge His people. He tempted David, the representative of the people, and David responded. God, already angry at some great sin of the people, moved David to continue on that path. It resulted in judgment on the very people God was angry at to begin with. In other words, the innocent sheep were actually not innocent after all; it was their own sin that led to their own judgment!

But the question that statement will produce is utterly predictable: "If this was all about the sin of the people, why even have David, the king, get involved?"

The answer is, from the devil's perspective, he desires to destroy everyone, from the king to the lowest servant in the field. But, and this will speak volumes to the true character of God, from God's perspective, this was all about giving his people a chance for someone to step in for them.

The obligation of the king and the people

After the sin of the people, God came to David and did something very unusual. He actually offered him a choice of punishments. And in that list of punishments there is an answer to a lot of questions. Look at the options God offered:

2 Samuel 24:12 *Go and say unto David, Thus saith the LORD, I offer thee three things; choose thee one of them, that I may do it unto thee. 13 So Gad came to David, and told him, and said unto him, Shall seven years of famine come unto thee in thy land? or wilt thou flee three months before thine enemies, while they pursue thee? or that there be three days' pestilence in thy land? now advise, and see what answer I shall return to him that sent me.*

There are the three options that God offered. But in the words of an old children's song, "One of these things is not like the other, one of these things is not the same..."

The first option was seven years of famine. How many people does a famine affect? Everyone.

The third option was three days pestilence in the land. That is a somewhat general term that indicates a disease or infestation that covers an entire land. How many people does that effect? Everyone.

But there is one person who would be much more insulated than others in those two judgments, and that would be the king. He would be the last one to ever starve, and he would have better care and protection in pestilence than anyone else.

There is one other judgment, though. And in that judgment, the pronouns are very prominent. Look at it again:

*"...or wilt **thou** flee three months before **thine** enemies, while they pursue **thee**?"*

Thee and thou in the Bible are second person **singular** pronouns. In other words, in this judgment God was offering David the opportunity to have to be on the run from his enemies for three months, God was offering David the ability to take the brunt of judgment for his people! In case you doubt that, you might want to pay attention to David actually admitting that very thing, and chose not to go that route:

2 Samuel 24:14 *And David said unto Gad, I am in a great strait: let **us** fall now into the hand of the LORD; for his mercies are great: and let **me** not fall into the hand of man.*

If you want to know why the people were judged, you will find that answer both in the fact that it was their sin that angered God to begin with and in the fact that their own king chose to let the hammer fall on them rather than take the punishment on himself.

How glad I am that we have a king who chose to do the exact opposite thing of David!

A summary of this is: One, the people were not innocent souls killed for David's sin. In fact, it was their sin that started the ball rolling. Two, David had a chance to spare his people but chose to sacrifice his people and spare himself. Three, the devil started the process, David went along with it, and then God greased the skids for the decision that had already been made. Four, David was a king who gave up his people to save himself, but Jesus is the King who gave up Himself to save His people!

Chapter Sixteen
Borrowing Trouble

Exodus 3:15 *And God said moreover unto Moses, Thus shalt thou say unto the children of Israel, The LORD God of your fathers, the God of Abraham, the God of Isaac, and the God of Jacob, hath sent me unto you: this is my name for ever, and this is my memorial unto all generations.* **16** *Go, and gather the elders of Israel together, and say unto them, The LORD God of your fathers, the God of Abraham, of Isaac, and of Jacob, appeared unto me, saying, I have surely visited you, and seen that which is done to you in Egypt:* **17** *And I have said, I will bring you up out of the affliction of Egypt unto the land of the Canaanites, and the Hittites, and the Amorites, and the Perizzites, and the Hivites, and the Jebusites, unto a land flowing with milk and honey.* **18** *And they shall hearken to thy voice: and thou shalt come, thou and the elders of Israel, unto the king of Egypt, and ye shall say unto him, The LORD God of the Hebrews hath met with us: and now let us go, we beseech thee, three days' journey into the wilderness, that we may sacrifice to the LORD our God.* **19** *And I am sure that the king of Egypt will not let you go, no, not by a mighty hand.* **20** *And I will stretch out my hand, and smite Egypt with all my wonders which I will do in the midst thereof: and after that he will let you go.* **21** *And I will give this people favour in the sight of the Egyptians: and it shall come to pass, that, when ye go, ye shall not go empty:*

22 *But every woman shall borrow of her neighbour, and of her that sojourneth in her house, jewels of silver, and jewels of gold, and raiment: and ye shall put them upon your sons, and upon your daughters; and ye shall spoil the Egyptians.*

Exodus 11:1 *And the LORD said unto Moses, Yet will I bring one plague more upon Pharaoh, and upon Egypt; afterwards he will let you go hence: when he shall let you go, he shall surely thrust you out hence altogether.* **2** *Speak now in the ears of the people, and let every man borrow of his neighbour, and every woman of her neighbour, jewels of silver, and jewels of gold.* **3** *And the LORD gave the people favour in the sight of the Egyptians. Moreover the man Moses was very great in the land of Egypt, in the sight of Pharaoh's servants, and in the sight of the people.*

Exodus 12:33 *And the Egyptians were urgent upon the people, that they might send them out of the land in haste; for they said, We be all dead men.* **34** *And the people took their dough before it was leavened, their kneadingtroughs being bound up in their clothes upon their shoulders.* **35** *And the children of Israel did according to the word of Moses; and they borrowed of the Egyptians jewels of silver, and jewels of gold, and raiment:* **36** *And the LORD gave the people favour in the sight of the Egyptians, so that they lent unto them such things as they required. And they spoiled the Egyptians.*

Psalm 37:21 *The wicked borroweth, and payeth not again: but the righteous sheweth mercy, and giveth.*

The perceived moral failing of God and His people in these texts is not something you have to look for with a microscope. It is so obvious that even as a child I wondered about it. God told His people to borrow things from the Egyptians, yet nowhere are we ever told that the borrowing was repaid. In fact, we are told that the Israelites "spoiled" the Egyptians, meaning that they "plundered" them. They took the items and left.

And yet, the same God that commanded that also authored the passage in Psalm 37:21 that says "The wicked borroweth, and payeth not again."

It certainly seems like if God and His people want to be regarded as just, they have just hurt themselves by "borrowing trouble!"

But, as has been the case in every single chapter, things are not what they seem on the surface.

The definition of borrow

I do not know how many of you have a Strong's Concordance, but it is a handy tool. You can look up a word, and it will list every time in the Bible it is used. Out beside each one, there will be a number. You can look at that number, go to the back of the book and find it, and it will tell you what Greek or Hebrew word it came from and what it means.

For a really in-depth study there are other things you can use that go much farther, but for the average person, it is all you will ever need.

One thing it will do is let you see if words in English came from the same word in Greek or Hebrew, and in this case, as I say so often, "One of these things is not like the other, one of these things is not the same."

In all three of the passages from Exodus, it comes from the word *sha-al*. In the passage from Psalms, it is from the word *lavah*. So even before you know what they mean, what do you already know? *They are different!* Whatever God was talking about in Psalm 37:21, that is not what He was talking about in the Exodus.

And, even before you define the words, just looking at the context of the verse in Psalms will tell you that it is borrowing in the typical, normally understood sense. Someone has borrowed, and they are expected to repay.

But if that word is different from the one in Exodus, then what does that tell you about the word in Exodus? It tells

219

you that that word is not to be regarded in that sense, it tells you that it means something completely different.

So, what does it mean?

Sha-al is used 173 times in the Old Testament. It means to ask, require, demand, desire. It is also such a versatile word that it is even used in one of the texts that we read a moment ago, Exodus 12:36, where it says "*And the LORD gave the people favour in the sight of the Egyptians, so that they **lent** unto them such things as they required.*" That word lent is the same word for borrow in the rest of the verses we are studying in Exodus. And in those texts, it means "borrow," not in the sense of "give me this and I will repay you," but simply in the sense of "I want that."

We still use that word like that. Many times at the table I will say, "Let me borrow the salt, please." I have no intention of repaying that salt; I intend to eat it.

Four hundred years ago when we were given our King James Bible, that was a fairly common way to use that word. It is not a bad translation, it is simply a word that we need to study and define. And if we do, we will learn that God was not dishonest, and His people were not dishonest, not in the least. When they spoke to the Egyptians, the Egyptians understood very clearly that what they were giving would never be returned or repaid, because the word *Sha-al* the Israelites used when talking to them made that very clear.

So, the biggest issue is settled. But there are still more things to learn.

The debt being settled

In America today, you will find people pushing for something called "reparations." In other words, there are a great many people that believe that because black people were once enslaved, their descendants should be given money or land today.

For what it is worth, I disagree with that for a number of reasons. But what I find really interesting is that it is normally liberals that push for that, and they are the very ones that take a passage like this and try to say that God and Israel did something wrong. But if there was ever a people that deserved some form of reparations, it was the Jews!

Consider the differences. With slaves in America, they were given their freedom, allowed to stay in the land, and they have become far wealthier and more successful than any of their relatives still in Africa. With the Jews, Egypt never would have let them be free in the land, and ended up throwing them out after using and abusing them for four hundred years. With slaves in America, a black man has now been voted into the highest office in our land. With the Jews in Egypt, there would never ever be a "Jewish Pharaoh." With slaves in America, they had people abusing them, with Jews in Egypt, they had the entire government at the very highest level not just abusing them but actually attempting genocide:

Exodus 1:22 *And Pharaoh charged all his people, saying, Every son that is born ye shall cast into the river, and every daughter ye shall save alive.*

How bad was it in Egypt? Twice Scripture calls it the "iron furnace." How bad was it in Egypt? A Jew saved their entire nation, and then they were enslaved, and all that Joseph had done was forgotten. Joseph saved Egypt, turned it into a world power, and then Joseph's people spent the next four hundred years as the worst treated slaves in history.

What did the Jewish slaves do for Egypt?

Exodus 1:11 *Therefore they did set over them taskmasters to afflict them with their burdens. **And they built for Pharaoh treasure cities, Pithom and Raamses.***

What I am saying is, there is no way possible that what they were given by the Egyptians in one night so much as even came close to settling the debt they were owed. Not only were God and Israel not dishonest, but Israel was also only being given a tiny fraction of what they were actually owed for what they were forced to produce for Egypt.

221

The divine provision being given

Exodus 12:35 *And the children of Israel did according to the word of Moses; and they borrowed of the Egyptians jewels of silver, and jewels of gold, and raiment:* **36 And the LORD gave the people favour in the sight of the Egyptians**, *so that they lent unto them such things as they required. And they spoiled the Egyptians.*

There are many miracles that happened during the time of the Exodus: the water turning to blood, the frogs, the flies, the lice, the fire and hail, the three days of darkness, the Passover, and many more. But there is one miracle that I have never heard labeled as a miracle, and this is it. God made the Egyptians love the Jews for one night, just long enough for them to give away all of their jewelry.

Look what happened right after this:

Exodus 14:5 *And it was told the king of Egypt that the people fled: and the heart of Pharaoh and of his servants was turned against the people, and they said, Why have we done this, that we have let Israel go from serving us?*

For one night, God did a miracle, a divine "love potion" in the hearts of the Egyptians. God miraculously provided for His people in what He did.

Think about it. An entire nation of two million people or more was about the be thrust out of the land into the desert. They were going to march through the desert and then have to fight their way into the Promised Land. My question is, with what money? They were not given wages as slaves. They were about to leave empty-handed, making it impossible to buy weapons or supplies. And then at the last moment, God did a "reaping and sowing miracle." Egypt had stolen from the Jews for four hundred years, and God made Egypt give the Jews all of their jewels and goodies before they left. That reminds me of something David the psalmist said many years later:

Psalm 23:5 *Thou preparest a table before me in the presence of mine enemies: thou anointest my head with oil; my cup runneth over.*

Do you know what you and I can learn from this, apart from the fact that neither God nor Israel did anything dishonest? We can learn that God provides for His own, and He often does so in a way that at least somewhat settles the score for previous wrongs.

God could have rained jewelry down from heaven on them. But tell me, which do you think the Jews would rather have had?

Never, ever forget: God can take care of you in ways that you could never even imagine ahead of time.

Chapter Seventeen
What's That on Your Pedestal?

For our text, though we are studying the Old Testament, we will be turning to the New Testament. It will quickly be evident why we are doing so.

Hebrews 11:7 *By faith Noah, being warned of God of things not seen as yet, moved with fear, prepared an ark to the saving of his house; by the which he condemned the world, and became heir of the righteousness which is by faith.* **8** *By faith Abraham, when he was called to go out into a place which he should after receive for an inheritance, obeyed; and he went out, not knowing whither he went.* **9** *By faith he sojourned in the land of promise, as in a strange country, dwelling in tabernacles with Isaac and Jacob, the heirs with him of the same promise:* **10** *For he looked for a city which hath foundations, whose builder and maker is God.* **11** *Through faith also Sara herself received strength to conceive seed, and was delivered of a child when she was past age, because she judged him faithful who had promised.* **12** *Therefore sprang there even of one, and him as good as dead, so many as the stars of the sky in multitude, and as the sand which is by the sea shore innumerable.* **13** *These all died in faith, not having received the promises, but having seen them afar off, and were persuaded of them, and embraced them, and confessed that they were strangers and pilgrims on the earth.* **14** *For they that say such things declare plainly*

225

that they seek a country. **15** *And truly, if they had been mindful of that country from whence they came out, they might have had opportunity to have returned.* **16** *But now they desire a better country, that is, an heavenly: wherefore God is not ashamed to be called their God: for he hath prepared for them a city.* **17** *By faith Abraham, when he was tried, offered up Isaac: and he that had received the promises offered up his only begotten son,* **18** *Of whom it was said, That in Isaac shall thy seed be called:* **19** *Accounting that God was able to raise him up, even from the dead; from whence also he received him in a figure.* **20** *By faith Isaac blessed Jacob and Esau concerning things to come.* **21** *By faith Jacob, when he was a dying, blessed both the sons of Joseph; and worshipped, leaning upon the top of his staff.* **22** *By faith Joseph, when he died, made mention of the departing of the children of Israel; and gave commandment concerning his bones.* **23** *By faith Moses, when he was born, was hid three months of his parents, because they saw he was a proper child; and they were not afraid of the king's commandment.* **24** *By faith Moses, when he was come to years, refused to be called the son of Pharaoh's daughter;* **25** *Choosing rather to suffer affliction with the people of God, than to enjoy the pleasures of sin for a season;* **26** *Esteeming the reproach of Christ greater riches than the treasures in Egypt: for he had respect unto the recompence of the reward.* **27** *By faith he forsook Egypt, not fearing the wrath of the king: for he endured, as seeing him who is invisible.* **28** *Through faith he kept the passover, and the sprinkling of blood, lest he that destroyed the firstborn should touch them.* **29** *By faith they passed through the Red sea as by dry land: which the Egyptians assaying to do were drowned.* **30** *By faith the walls of Jericho fell down, after they were compassed about seven days.* **31** *By faith the harlot Rahab perished not with them that believed not, when she had received the spies with peace.* **32** *And what shall I more say? for the time would fail me to tell of Gedeon, and of Barak,* *and of Samson, and of Jephthae; of David also, and Samuel, and of the prophets: **33** Who through faith subdued kingdoms, wrought righteousness, obtained promises, stopped the mouths of lions, **34** Quenched the violence of fire, escaped the edge of the sword, out of weakness were made strong, waxed valiant in fight, turned to flight the armies of the aliens.*

Hebrews 11 is a summary chapter listing a great many of the superstars of the Old Testament. Let me give you the names of several of them:

Noah, Abraham, Isaac, Jacob, Moses, Gideon, Samson, David, Samuel. All of these are listed as great men of faith.

Now let me add some names of other "heroes" that did not even make this list: Lot, Jonah, Solomon, Judah, Aaron.

All of these men are "up on a pedestal," if you will. And that brings us to what seems to be a bit of a conundrum. Let's examine it.

The wicked behavior of Biblical heroes

When we begin to examine the lives of the "heroes of the faith," if we are honest, we will have to admit that when the scoffers look at these men and view them largely as scoundrels, they are right! Consider:

Noah got drunk out of his mind.

Abraham, whom the book of James called the "friend of God," the man who founded the Jewish nation, the man through whom all of the promises came, lied about his wife, twice. Twice he told other men that Sarah was his sister. Twice he watched as other men led his wife away to their house. Twice!

Lot, whom the New Testament describes as a "righteous" man, offered his own two virgin daughters to a bunch of perverted men to abuse!

Isaac, the promised seed, lied about his wife being his sister too.

Jacob was one of the greatest liars and con artists of all time. In our day he would be convicted of multiple felonies and sent to prison for a very long time.

Judah, the founder of the tribe Jesus came from, slept with a harlot who just so happened to be his own daughter in law.

Moses the great deliverer, the man who spoke with God face to face, revered by Jews to this very day, murdered a man. His brother Aaron, the first high priest, made an idol for the people to worship. The great judge Gideon did very much the same thing.

Do we really even need to elaborate on Samson? Hardly an example you want to encourage members of your youth group to aspire to be like.

Samuel did not even bother to raise his own sons for God.

David, whom God once called a man after His own heart, stole one of his best friend's wives, committed adultery with her, and then murdered his friend to cover it up.

Solomon was perhaps the greatest womanizer ever.

Jonah, a prophet of God, actually wanted a city full of hundreds of thousands of people to die and go to hell.

The scoffer sees this and says, "This is the God you serve, the God who has these men as His golden boys?" And do you know what? If we are going to be what we wish they were, honest, we have to admit that the great heroes of the faith were, by and large, some really terrible people at times.

Reading your Old Testament honestly will often result in you wanting to reach into the pages and grab these men by the collar and shake them. There is absolutely no reason to deny that.

The writing verified by wicked heroes

There is not just a silver lining to the wicked behavior of heroes in the Bible, there is actually a solid gold lining to it, one that has to do with the Bible itself.

There is a principle that textual critics will use to help them decide if an ancient writing is likely to be true. It is called the embarrassment principle or the principle of dissimilarity. It basically means that the more embarrassing an account is to the author, the more likely it is to be true.

You see, an author has "omnipotent power" over the text. That being the case, he has the ability to make himself look as good as he desires. If I write my own autobiography, I can promise you that there are things I would be very tempted to leave out of it. And I can also promise you that if any of you ever write your autobiography, there are things you would be tempted to leave out as well.

But when we come to the Bible, we have God holding up a bunch of men as heroes of the faith, and then listing every awful thing they ever did. Do you know what this means? It means you can trust that your Bible is authentic and true. There has been no effort made to "sanitize" things. People are shown warts and all.

If any man or men authored the Bible, this is not how it would be written. Every man would be brave; Gideon would not be hiding behind the winepress, and Barak would not be refusing to go to war unless Deborah comes with him. Every husband would be loyal and romantic, and none of them would be waving goodbye to their wives whom they had just lied about and called their sisters. None of them would be murderers. Lot would not be included in the writing, at all, ever.

Were the "heroes of the faith" some of the most motley scoundrels ever? Yes, yes they were. The Bible is utterly honest in everything, including in its portrayal of its heroes.

The greatest thing about all of the stupidity and sin that you read about in the lives of these men is that it is an incredibly strong verification that you can trust your Bible.

The work in progress of Biblical heroes

One thing we should always do when evaluating people is to find out what they had to work with as far as their character went. It is very easy for the scoffer especially to rail on the patriarchs, but even though we have rightly labeled their behavior as wicked, we can only be truly fair to them by pointing out that we are far more blessed than they were by some things.

What Scripture did Abraham, Isaac, and Jacob have to mold and shape them? None. They also did not have any support system around them to help either. Abraham was, in his day, the original monotheist. He stepped out and followed God when the entire rest of the world was going a different direction.

Not one person in the entire Old Testament had all of Scripture to work with. The behavior that Abraham and others demonstrated fit in with many men of their time. That does not make it right, but it should make us pause just a bit before we lambast them. How well would we do, any of us, if we lived when and where they did and were in the exact same situations they were in? We have learned from their mistakes; they did not have a similar luxury.

The worthwhile things they did before and after their wickedness

Abraham? Despite his undeniable wrong doing, he also showed a faith that surpasses most any that the world has ever seen. Samson, despite squandering a lifetime of strength and potential, still managed to do at his death what he was supposed to have done in his life. Jacob, despite being a liar and a con-artist, got serious enough with God for God to change his name from one that meant "con artist" to one that meant "prince." Moses, despite having a murder charge laid at his feet, went on to serve God in the most extraordinary fashion for eighty solid years. Never forget that, since God does not have anyone perfect to work with, He delights in bringing greatness out of the least likely sources.

The wonder of them being regarded as heroes

There are two different approaches you can take when considering this subject. One, you can decide that God is somehow immoral by having these men as His examples to hold up to us. Or, what you could do is jump up and down and shout for joy once you really figure out what God is up to.

There is a word that occurs one hundred and seventy times in the Bible. It is, in fact, at the very heart of the entire message of the Bible. It is first found in Genesis 6:8:

Genesis 6:8 *But Noah found grace in the eyes of the LORD.*

Grace, God's unmerited favor toward man. Grace, God giving us the good things we do not deserve. Grace, God condescending to men of low estate.

You see, the point of Scripture is not the men of God, but the God of the men, who just so happens to be the God of grace.

Do you know what? You are not supposed to look at Abraham and give him a pass for passing off his wife. You are supposed to look at Abraham and say, "God, I can think of a lot of times I have lied too, and I can think of a lot of times I was not all that I should be for my spouse. You gave Abraham grace, thank you for doing the same for me."

You are not supposed to look at Jacob and admire the fact that he was a liar and con artist. You are supposed to look at Jacob and admire the God who gave him grace when he needed it because that is the same God that gives you grace when you need it.

We could go down the list on each and every one. The fact that the Bible records their misdeeds and then shows God blessing them anyway is a testimony to the grace of God. People who have cursed or looked at pornography or stolen or gossiped or lied need to not be hard on those men; God died to pay for everything they did and everything we did.

One day we are going to get to heaven and have God look us in the eyes and say, "Well done, good and faithful servant." And when we do, that great cloud of witnesses, Abraham, Jacob, etc., those men who watched while we stumbled and fell just like they stumbled and fell, are going to smile at us and have one word forming on their smiling lips:

Grace.

What's that on your pedestal? Just a bunch of trophies, trophies of grace.

Chapter Eighteen
An Unholy Alliance?

1 Kings 22:1 *And they continued three years without war between Syria and Israel.* **2** *And it came to pass in the third year, that Jehoshaphat the king of Judah came down to the king of Israel.* **3** *And the king of Israel said unto his servants, Know ye that Ramoth in Gilead is ours, and we be still, and take it not out of the hand of the king of Syria?* **4** *And he said unto Jehoshaphat, Wilt thou go with me to battle to Ramothgilead? And Jehoshaphat said to the king of Israel, I am as thou art, my people as thy people, my horses as thy horses.* **5** *And Jehoshaphat said unto the king of Israel, Enquire, I pray thee, at the word of the LORD to day.* **6** *Then the king of Israel gathered the prophets together, about four hundred men, and said unto them, Shall I go against Ramothgilead to battle, or shall I forbear? And they said, Go up; for the Lord shall deliver it into the hand of the king.* **7** *And Jehoshaphat said, Is there not here a prophet of the LORD besides, that we might enquire of him?* **8** *And the king of Israel said unto Jehoshaphat, There is yet one man, Micaiah the son of Imlah, by whom we may enquire of the LORD: but I hate him; for he doth not prophesy good concerning me, but evil. And Jehoshaphat said, Let not the king say so.* **9** *Then the king of Israel called an officer, and said, Hasten hither Micaiah the son of Imlah.* **10** *And the king of Israel and Jehoshaphat the king of Judah sat each on his* *throne, having put on their robes, in a void place in the entrance of the gate of Samaria; and all the prophets prophesied before them.* **11** *And Zedekiah the son of Chenaanah made him horns of iron: and he said, Thus saith the LORD, With these shalt thou push the Syrians, until thou have consumed them.* **12** *And all the prophets prophesied so, saying, Go up to Ramothgilead, and prosper: for the LORD shall deliver it into the king's hand.* **13** *And the messenger that was gone to call Micaiah spake unto him, saying, Behold now, the words of the prophets declare good unto the king with one mouth: let thy word, I pray thee, be like the word of one of them, and speak that which is good.* **14** *And Micaiah said, As the LORD liveth, what the LORD saith unto me, that will I speak.* **15** *So he came to the king. And the king said unto him, Micaiah, shall we go against Ramothgilead to battle, or shall we forbear? And he answered him, Go, and prosper: for the LORD shall deliver it into the hand of the king.* **16** *And the king said unto him, How many times shall I adjure thee that thou tell me nothing but that which is true in the name of the LORD?* **17** *And he said, I saw all Israel scattered upon the hills, as sheep that have not a shepherd: and the LORD said, These have no master: let them return every man to his house in peace.* **18** *And the king of Israel said unto Jehoshaphat, Did I not tell thee that he would prophesy no good concerning me, but evil?* **19** *And he said, Hear thou therefore the word of the LORD: I saw the LORD sitting on his throne, and all the host of heaven standing by him on his right hand and on his left.* **20** *And the LORD said, Who shall persuade Ahab, that he may go up and fall at Ramothgilead? And one said on this manner, and another said on that manner.* **21** *And there came forth a spirit, and stood before the LORD, and said, I will persuade him.* **22** *And the LORD said unto him, Wherewith? And he said, I will go forth, and I will be a lying spirit in the mouth of all his prophets. And he said, Thou shalt persuade him, and prevail also: go forth, and do so.* **23** *Now therefore, behold, the LORD hath put a lying* *spirit in the mouth of all these thy prophets, and the LORD hath spoken evil concerning thee. 24 But Zedekiah the son of Chenaanah went near, and smote Micaiah on the cheek, and said, Which way went the Spirit of the LORD from me to speak unto thee? 25 And Micaiah said, Behold, thou shalt see in that day, when thou shalt go into an inner chamber to hide thyself. 26 And the king of Israel said, Take Micaiah, and carry him back unto Amon the governor of the city, and to Joash the king's son; 27 And say, Thus saith the king, Put this fellow in the prison, and feed him with bread of affliction and with water of affliction, until I come in peace. 28 And Micaiah said, If thou return at all in peace, the LORD hath not spoken by me. And he said, Hearken, O people, every one of you. 29 So the king of Israel and Jehoshaphat the king of Judah went up to Ramothgilead. 30 And the king of Israel said unto Jehoshaphat, I will disguise myself, and enter into the battle; but put thou on thy robes. And the king of Israel disguised himself, and went into the battle. 31 But the king of Syria commanded his thirty and two captains that had rule over his chariots, saying, Fight neither with small nor great, save only with the king of Israel. 32 And it came to pass, when the captains of the chariots saw Jehoshaphat, that they said, Surely it is the king of Israel. And they turned aside to fight against him: and Jehoshaphat cried out. 33 And it came to pass, when the captains of the chariots perceived that it was not the king of Israel, that they turned back from pursuing him. 34 And a certain man drew a bow at a venture, and smote the king of Israel between the joints of the harness: wherefore he said unto the driver of his chariot, Turn thine hand, and carry me out of the host; for I am wounded. 35 And the battle increased that day: and the king was stayed up in his chariot against the Syrians, and died at even: and the blood ran out of the wound into the midst of the chariot. 36 And there went a proclamation throughout the host about the going down of the sun, saying, Every man to his city, and every man to his own country. 37 So the king died, and was brought to Samaria; and they buried the king in Samaria.* **38** *And one washed the chariot in the pool of Samaria; and the dogs licked up his blood; and they washed his armour; according unto the word of the LORD which he spake.* **39** *Now the rest of the acts of Ahab, and all that he did, and the ivory house which he made, and all the cities that he built, are they not written in the book of the chronicles of the kings of Israel?* **40** *So Ahab slept with his fathers; and Ahaziah his son reigned in his stead.*

The text before us is one of the most unusual ones in the entire Bible. The most jaw-dropping portion of it is the recounting of a scene in heaven in which God seems to be commissioning a spirit, a demon, to go and speak lying words through the mouth of false prophets. This cannot help but make people wonder, whose side is God on? Is He allied with devils? The scoffer would surely love to be able to argue that point in the affirmative.

Let us dig into this text and find out what is happening and what we are to learn from it.

An Unholy Alliance

1 Kings 22:1 *And they continued three years without war between Syria and Israel.* **2** *And it came to pass in the third year, that Jehoshaphat the king of Judah came down to the king of Israel.* **3** *And the king of Israel said unto his servants, Know ye that Ramoth in Gilead is ours, and we be still, and take it not out of the hand of the king of Syria?* **4** *And he said unto Jehoshaphat, Wilt thou go with me to battle to Ramothgilead? And Jehoshaphat said to the king of Israel, I am as thou art, my people as thy people, my horses as thy horses.*

"It was singular that a friendly league between the sovereigns of Israel and Judah should, for the first time, have been formed by princes of such opposite characters—the one pious, the other wicked." (Jamison, 1:365)

This kind of thing is never a good idea for the godly party. A godly king was joining into an alliance with a wicked and debauched king. Look at what the New Testament instructs concerning that kind of thing:

2 Corinthians 6:14 *Be ye not unequally yoked together with unbelievers: for what fellowship hath righteousness with unrighteousness? and what communion hath light with darkness?*

2 Corinthians 6:17 *Wherefore come out from among them, and be ye separate, saith the Lord, and touch not the unclean thing; and I will receive you,* **18** *And will be a Father unto you, and ye shall be my sons and daughters, saith the Lord Almighty.*

Jehoshaphat was not entering into a "tentative, temporary alliance." His words tell us that he was joining lock, stock, and barrel with a man he should have been having nothing to do with. He was thinking in terms of political and national power and selling out what was right. Just like what we almost always see today.

Wrong is not going to drift toward the right by right drifting toward wrong. Wrong is going to go the way that it always does, and if you move toward it, you are going the wrong way for no good reason.

An Uneasy Feeling

1 Kings 22:5 *And Jehoshaphat said unto the king of Israel, Enquire, I pray thee, at the word of the LORD to day.* **6** *Then the king of Israel gathered the prophets together, about four hundred men, and said unto them, Shall I go against Ramothgilead to battle, or shall I forbear? And they said, Go up; for the Lord shall deliver it into the hand of the king.* **7** *And Jehoshaphat said, Is there not here a prophet of the LORD besides, that we might enquire of him?*

Twice in these verses Jehoshaphat demonstrates a great deal of uneasiness: once that leads him to ask for a prophet to come and once when he then asks for a *real* prophet to come! There is a difference between a "prophet" and a "prophet of the Lord." Jehoshaphat, despite his poor judgment on allies, seemed to have still had enough sense to realize that these self-styled prophets were more like "profiteers."

An Unbending Prophet

1 Kings 22:8 *And the king of Israel said unto Jehoshaphat, There is yet one man, Micaiah the son of Imlah, by whom we may enquire of the LORD: but I hate him; for he doth not prophesy good concerning me, but evil. And Jehoshaphat said, Let not the king say so.* **9** *Then the king of Israel called an officer, and said, Hasten hither Micaiah the son of Imlah.* **10** *And the king of Israel and Jehoshaphat the king of Judah sat each on his throne, having put on their robes, in a void place in the entrance of the gate of Samaria; and all the prophets prophesied before them.* **11** *And Zedekiah the son of Chenaanah made him horns of iron: and he said, Thus saith the LORD, With these shalt thou push the Syrians, until thou have consumed them.* **12** *And all the prophets prophesied so, saying, Go up to Ramothgilead, and prosper: for the LORD shall deliver it into the king's hand.* **13** *And the messenger that was gone to call Micaiah spake unto him, saying, Behold now, the words of the prophets declare good unto the king with one mouth: let thy word, I pray thee, be like the word of one of them, and speak that which is good.* **14** *And Micaiah said, As the LORD liveth, what the LORD saith unto me, that will I speak.* **15** *So he came to the king. And the king said unto him, Micaiah, shall we go against Ramothgilead to battle, or shall we forbear? And he answered him, Go, and prosper: for the LORD shall deliver it into the hand of the king.* **16** *And the king said unto him, How many times shall I adjure thee that thou tell me nothing but that which is true in the name of the LORD?* **17** *And he said, I saw all Israel scattered upon the hills, as sheep that have not a shepherd: and the LORD said, These have no master: let* *them return every man to his house in peace. 18 And the king of Israel said unto Jehoshaphat, Did I not tell thee that he would prophesy no good concerning me, but evil?*

When Micaiah came before the kings, he initially answered with an all too obvious sarcasm. That led to the wicked king of Israel exploding in anger and demanding that he tell the truth. Sad that he should ask that, since he clearly did not really want it.

Micaiah complied and gave a message of judgment and destruction from God. He could have feigned sincerity and safely joined the majority opinion, but his regard for God and truth was too high for that.

An Unusual Arrangement

1 Kings 22:19 *And he said, Hear thou therefore the word of the LORD: I saw the LORD sitting on his throne, and all the host of heaven standing by him on his right hand and on his left. 20 And the LORD said, Who shall persuade Ahab, that he may go up and fall at Ramothgilead? And one said on this manner, and another said on that manner. 21 And there came forth a spirit, and stood before the LORD, and said, I will persuade him. 22 And the LORD said unto him, Wherewith? And he said, I will go forth, and I will be a lying spirit in the mouth of all his prophets. And he said, Thou shalt persuade him, and prevail also: go forth, and do so. 23 Now therefore, behold, the LORD hath put a lying spirit in the mouth of all these thy prophets, and the LORD hath spoken evil concerning thee.*

Though the only unholy alliance in this text is that between two men, two kings, Jehoshaphat and Ahab, what we find here between God and these spirits at least qualifies as an unusual arrangement. Simply put, we do not find anything quite exactly like this in the rest of Scripture, other than this exact same event recorded in the parallel passage of 2 Chronicles 18. It is so unusual that commentator Adam Clarke tried to explain it away:

"This is a mere parable, and only tells in figurative language, what was in the womb of providence, the events which were shortly to take place, the agents employed in them, and the permission on the part of God for these agents to act. Micaiah did not choose to say before this angry and impious king, 'Thy prophets are all liars; and the devil, the father of lies, dwells in them;' but he represents the whole by this parable, and says the same truths in language as forcible, but less offensive." (2:476)

With all due respect, that is one of the most ridiculous things I have ever read. Consider it carefully: he says that the prophet used symbolism to tell the truth in a "less offensive way."

Tell me, which is less "offensive:" being told that you are a liar, or being told that you are a demon-possessed liar? What Micaiah said was not less offensive, it was MORE offensive. So why did he say it? For one reason only: it was true.

So, since it was true, since it really happened, how do we explain it? And did God somehow do wrong by utilizing demons to cause these false prophets to lie? And why would they want to help anyway? What is going on?

We need to begin by pointing out that this is not where everything started. The scene we see in heaven is the end of the story of Ahab. The scene where demons, those spirits on the left hand of the Lord intend to overthrow Ahab, is the end of the story. The scene where the angels, holy spirits on the right stand silent and allow it to happen, is the end of the story.

Ahab had been king under the ministry of the greatest of all prophets, Elijah. He had then continued to be king under Micaiah. Think of all of the "persuading" he received under Elijah, and yet he never gave up his wicked ways.

240

God will not woo forever. There will come a time when He stops drawing with the Holy Spirit. At that time, a person may well find him or herself drawn by a very unholy spirit:

John 13:21 *When Jesus had thus said, he was troubled in spirit, and testified, and said, Verily, verily, I say unto you, that one of you shall betray me.* **22** *Then the disciples looked one on another, doubting of whom he spake.* **23** *Now there was leaning on Jesus' bosom one of his disciples, whom Jesus loved.* **24** *Simon Peter therefore beckoned to him, that he should ask who it should be of whom he spake.* **25** *He then lying on Jesus' breast saith unto him, Lord, who is it?* **26** *Jesus answered, He it is, to whom I shall give a sop, when I have dipped it. And when he had dipped the sop, he gave it to Judas Iscariot, the son of Simon.* **27** *And after the sop Satan entered into him. Then said Jesus unto him, That thou doest, do quickly.*

Judas had three years of being wooed by the Son of God and the Holy Spirit. After pushing that away, he found himself under the control of the devil himself.

Ahab pushed God away as hard as he could. Finally, there came a time when God determined to end his life. Could He have simply spoken the word? Certainly. But just as He allows us to be used, He also allows spirits to be used. And in this instance, knowing that Ahab's life was about to be over, the devils of hell, who had delighted in using him, now turned on him like a pack of jackals and took pleasure in destroying him.

There are some things to learn from this.

One, learn that this is exactly how the devil is.

Two, learn that there are very real lying spirits, capable of getting a lot of people to tell the same lie.

Three, learn that God is God. In other words, be very careful about making statements that limit Him. For instance, I have heard all my life, "God cannot use an unclean vessel." The only problem with that is He does it all the time!

241

Samson... these devils... Balaam (the prophecy of the star came from his lips!)

God would rather use a clean vessel because He would rather that every vessel be clean. But God is so much God that He will use whatever He chooses, and we do not have the ability to box Him into our pet preferences.

Chapter Nineteen
The Deity of Dollars?

Exodus 30:11 *And the LORD spake unto Moses, saying,* **12** *When thou takest the sum of the children of Israel after their number, then shall they give every man a ransom for his soul unto the LORD, when thou numberest them; that there be no plague among them, when thou numberest them.* **13** *This they shall give, every one that passeth among them that are numbered, half a shekel after the shekel of the sanctuary: (a shekel is twenty gerahs:) an half shekel shall be the offering of the LORD.* **14** *Every one that passeth among them that are numbered, from twenty years old and above, shall give an offering unto the LORD.* **15** *The rich shall not give more, and the poor shall not give less than half a shekel, when they give an offering unto the LORD, to make an atonement for your souls.* **16** *And thou shalt take the atonement money of the children of Israel, and shalt appoint it for the service of the tabernacle of the congregation; that it may be a memorial unto the children of Israel before the LORD, to make an atonement for your souls.*

A very good, smart man, a lawyer, once asked me about the relationship between God and money in the Old Testament. It seemed to him that there was a lot to be said about money in the Old Testament. And he is correct, there is. Here is a partial list of words that are currency related and how many times they occur in the Old Testament:

243

Money - 117
Gold - 391
Silver - 302
Shekel - 43
Shekels - 96
Tithe - 12
Tithes - 18
Tithing - 2
Offering - 713
Offerings - 260

Keep in mind that there are other words and phrases we could look to. But just in those few words, we have instances in which money is somehow referenced in the Old Testament, and a great many of those relate to God commanding that His people bring it to Him. Most of the references to offerings were animals that were to be brought to sacrifice, but even those were a form of currency in those days.

In years gone by, before the advent of the modern prosperity gospel preacher, that really did not raise many eyebrows with anyone. People knew that God had been good to us and that He allowed us to have a part in His work by bringing offerings. But now, with the Creflo Dollars of the world trying to bilk gullible followers out of sixty-five million dollars to buy a "luxury jet for Jesus" to fly back and forth between mansions, the references to money in the Bible suddenly become a target.

But there is really no need to raise so much as a single eyebrow. Let me demonstrate this by asking and answering several questions about money from the Old Testament. When we are finished, you will once again see that the character of God stands sure.

Was money any kind of an actual benefit to God?

Just on a logical, sensible level alone this question is incredibly easy to answer. How can the God who created and owns the entire universe be benefitted by our trinkets?

Psalm 50:7 *Hear, O my people, and I will speak; O Israel, and I will testify against thee: I am God, even thy God.* **8** *I will not reprove thee for thy sacrifices or thy burnt offerings, to have been continually before me.* **9** *I will take no bullock out of thy house, nor he goats out of thy folds.* **10** *For every beast of the forest is mine, and the cattle upon a thousand hills.* **11** *I know all the fowls of the mountains: and the wild beasts of the field are mine.* **12** *If I were hungry, I would not tell thee: for the world is mine, and the fulness thereof.*

If the world is God's, if the fullness of the world, meaning everything in it is God's, then everything we give Him is already His anyway. So how can we benefit God by giving Him what is already His anyway?

From the time my children were very small, we taught them to give. Tithers do not happen by accident, they happen by parental training. Very often though, a unique thing took place. I preach a great many revival meetings. At those meetings, sometimes a love offering is taken up to help cover my expenses in being there. I say "sometimes" because there are actually quite a few times when I have preached different places and received nothing.

But during those meetings where love offerings were taken, my little children would often see the plate coming, and, realizing they had nothing to give (since those lazy little toddlers were unemployed and wholly dependent upon us for every need of life) they would look over to me and smile, and hold out their hand. I would pull out my wallet, give them each some money, and they would beam from ear to ear as they put that money in the plate.

There was no actual benefit to me in what my children gave. None. The only ones that gained any benefit were my children, they gained the joy of participating in the offering! I gave it to them, they gave it to the church which gave it right back to me.

That is a near flawless picture of the relationship in the Bible between God, His people, and money. Everything He asks us to give, He gives to us first, then we get the joy of giving it back.

Salstrand, in his book *The Tithe*, quotes David McConoughy, in *Money, The Acid Test*. "God has no need of the gifts of men; in fact, it is impossible for men to give to God except indirectly in ministering to the needs of His children... Giving is not for God's benefit but for our own... God knows that the only way to make His people like Himself is to develop in them His own unselfishness." (12)

Were God's people "burdened down" by excessive requirements of giving?

There are, as we have observed, hundreds of mentions of money and giving. But the regular giving required by the law actually fits into just three categories of tithing.

The first tenth that they were required to give was the produce of the land:

Leviticus 27:30 *And all the tithe of the land, whether of the seed of the land, or of the fruit of the tree, is the LORD'S: it is holy unto the LORD. 31 And if a man will at all redeem ought of his tithes, he shall add thereto the fifth part thereof. 32 And concerning the tithe of the herd, or of the flock, even of whatsoever passeth under the rod, the tenth shall be holy unto the LORD. 33 He shall not search whether it be good or bad, neither shall he change it: and if he change it at all, then both it and the change thereof shall be holy; it shall not be redeemed.*

The most common currency of the day was crops and livestock. This passage tells us that they were to give a tenth of all of the crops and livestock, and that if they for whatever reason wanted to keep a certain part of the crops, maybe because those particular ears of corn were literally the best tasting ones ever, they would give that amount of money plus twenty percent more of its value.

To illustrate, if for some reason a man had $1000 worth of wheat, and rather than give a tenth of that particular batch as tithe he needed to keep it and use it, he could simply give the tithe of $100 plus another $20 and keep the wheat.

According to Numbers 18:21-24, this particular tithe was used for the maintenance of the ministry. The Levites, the men of God, lived off of that income as they served the Lord full time.

The second tithe was often called the festival tithe:

Deuteronomy 14:22 *Thou shalt truly tithe all the increase of thy seed, that the field bringeth forth year by year.* **23** *And thou shalt eat before the LORD thy God, in the place which he shall choose to place his name there, the tithe of thy corn, of thy wine, and of thine oil, and the firstlings of thy herds and of thy flocks; that thou mayest learn to fear the LORD thy God always.* **24** *And if the way be too long for thee, so that thou art not able to carry it; or if the place be too far from thee, which the LORD thy God shall choose to set his name there, when the LORD thy God hath blessed thee:* **25** *Then shalt thou turn it into money, and bind up the money in thine hand, and shalt go unto the place which the LORD thy God shall choose:* **26** *And thou shalt bestow that money for whatsoever thy soul lusteth after, for oxen, or for sheep, or for wine, or for strong drink, or for whatsoever thy soul desireth: and thou shalt eat there before the LORD thy God, and thou shalt rejoice, thou, and thine household,* **27** *And the Levite that is within thy gates; thou shalt not forsake him; for he hath no part nor inheritance with thee.*

This tenth went to what amounted to a family holiday in the Lord's house. They could not take it to the beach or the fair, it had to be brought to the house of worship. But once it was brought there, it was used for a feast of celebration. This occurred during the Passover, the Feast of Tabernacles, and the Feast of Weeks. Three celebrations in a year, all involving worship. The nearest parallel we likely have to that today is when we go to church camp meetings.

There was a third tithe, a third tenth. Unlike the other two yearly tithes, this one occurred every third year:

Deuteronomy 14:28 *At the end of three years thou shalt bring forth all the tithe of thine increase the same year, and shalt lay it up within thy gates:* **29** *And the Levite, (because he hath no part nor inheritance with thee,) and the stranger, and the fatherless, and the widow, which are within thy gates, shall come, and shall eat and be satisfied; that the LORD thy God may bless thee in all the work of thine hand which thou doest.*

This tithe was used specifically to meet the needs of the less fortunate. Both Josephus and the book of Tobit mentioned this third tithe.

So, when you run the numbers, you find that the children of Israel gave ten percent a year to the upkeep of the ministry, ten percent a year to fund celebrations of worship that they went to, and three and a third percent a year to meet the needs of the poor. Twenty-three and a third percent of their income.

This does not include the sacrifices and offerings for sin they made, and a shekel here and there for other things, but those were not a large expenditure at all, so just figure twenty-five percent or less of their income.

But in addition to that, they also from time to time did as we still do and took up a special offering for some special need. Let me show you the most famous of these.

Exodus 36:1 *Then wrought Bezaleel and Aholiab, and every wise hearted man, in whom the LORD put wisdom and understanding to know how to work all manner of work for the service of the sanctuary, according to all that the LORD had commanded.* **2** *And Moses called Bezaleel and Aholiab, and every wise hearted man, in whose heart the LORD had put wisdom, even every one whose heart stirred him up to* come unto the work to do it: *3 And they received of Moses all the offering, which the children of Israel had brought for the work of the service of the sanctuary, to make it withal. And they brought yet unto him free offerings every morning. 4 And all the wise men, that wrought all the work of the sanctuary, came every man from his work which they made; 5 And they spake unto Moses, saying, The people bring much more than enough for the service of the work, which the LORD commanded to make. 6 And Moses gave commandment, and they caused it to be proclaimed throughout the camp, saying, Let neither man nor woman make any more work for the offering of the sanctuary. So the people were restrained from bringing. 7 For the stuff they had was sufficient for all the work to make it, and too much.*

This offering shows the heartbeat of God and His people on the matter and also answers our question as to whether the people were overburdened with having to give. Moses called for a special offering to build the tabernacle, and it was completely voluntary in nature. The people freely gave so much that they had to be restrained from bringing anything else!

No, the people were not overburdened with giving. God took them from slavery, gave them a land complete with houses already built and fields already sown, and they prospered under the system He gave them.

Did Old Testament ministers (priests, prophets) live lavishly?

Not even close. In fact, the Levites were the only tribe that was not a land holding tribe with their own area of the land. They were given cities within the other tribe's land.

Numbers 35:1 *And the LORD spake unto Moses in the plains of Moab by Jordan near Jericho, saying, 2 Command the children of Israel, that they give unto the Levites of the inheritance of their possession cities to dwell in; and ye shall give also unto the Levites suburbs for the*

249

cities round about them. 3 And the cities shall they have to dwell in; and the suburbs of them shall be for their cattle, and for their goods, and for all their beasts. 4 And the suburbs of the cities, which ye shall give unto the Levites, shall reach from the wall of the city and outward a thousand cubits round about. 5 And ye shall measure from without the city on the east side two thousand cubits, and on the south side two thousand cubits, and on the west side two thousand cubits, and on the north side two thousand cubits; and the city shall be in the midst: this shall be to them the suburbs of the cities.

The priests who ministered in the tabernacle were allowed to eat certain parts of the meat offered before the Lord. The Levites had their cities to live in. But nothing in the entire system of giving laid out in the law made them rich. Nothing in the system of giving even mentioned the prophets, either, we find them sometimes receiving offerings from others for what they did, sometimes not, and sometimes even refusing what had been offered.

What did all of that money go for?

As we have previously noted, ten percent went to the upkeep of the ministry, ten percent to family celebrations during religious festivals, and ten percent every third year to what we would call charity.

The only question then becomes what was done with the first tenth. We saw that it was basically the paycheck for the priests and Levites and the upkeep of the house of God.

The house of God itself was built with that special offering we noted from Exodus 36. It was then maintained by that first tenth. There were no churches on every corner during the period of the law, there was just the tabernacle, and it served as the center of worship for multiple millions of people. That multi-million-member tabernacle and the men of God that served it were what "all that money" went for. If this were a simple church we were talking about, there might be cause for a raised eyebrow or two, but with the entire nation worshiping in the same place, it makes perfect sense.

Did that money ever ostensibly "buy salvation?"

There is one passage that, more than most, makes people wonder about the character of God when it came to money in the Old Testament:

Exodus 30:11 *And the LORD spake unto Moses, saying,* **12** *When thou takest the sum of the children of Israel after their number, then shall they give every man a ransom for his soul unto the LORD, when thou numberest them; that there be no plague among them, when thou numberest them.* **13** *This they shall give, every one that passeth among them that are numbered, half a shekel after the shekel of the sanctuary: (a shekel is twenty gerahs:) an half shekel shall be the offering of the LORD.* **14** *Every one that passeth among them that are numbered, from twenty years old and above, shall give an offering unto the LORD.* **15** *The rich shall not give more, and the poor shall not give less than half a shekel, when they give an offering unto the LORD, to make an atonement for your souls.*

When we see the words "ransom for his soul," and then see it followed by "that there be no plague among them," and then see the phrase "atonement for your souls," it is evident that we better slow down and figure out what is going on.

According to verse sixteen, this was used for the service of the tabernacle, so what it went for is legitimate and does not raise a question.

It is also in verse sixteen that we find a word that is key to understanding the theological question raised by this passage. This was to be done as a "memorial." In other words, the atonement spoken of was not "them getting saved by giving," it was them giving in remembrance of their previous deliverance, specifically from Egypt.

251

Would there be a plague on those who refused to give? Yes. This was a commemoration of the most important thing that ever happened to Israel. The first generation would never forget it, they lived it. But every other generation would forget it unless there was something very serious reminding them of it, and this was it.

As to the amount given, there are two significant things to note. One, it was not very much money at all, maybe five or ten dollars in today's money based on the fluctuating value of silver. In other words, this was not a burden, anyone could afford this once a year coin. Two, the rich could not give more, the poor could not give less.

Why was that? Because it was a ransom for souls, and every soul was equally valuable. For the rich to be allowed to give more would send the message that their soul was more important than the soul of the poor, and for the poor to be allowed to give less would indicate that their soul was worth less than the soul of the rich.

But none of it bought salvation. The punishment for disobeying was not hell, but a physical plague.

Why did God have so much to say about money?

I will quote George Salstrand on this, I believe he perfectly sums it up.

"A discussion of tithe-giving is important because with too many people giving is only a matter of impulse. As long as God's people give by impulse rather than principle the cause of Jesus Christ will continue to suffer and languish." (14)

That is a good summary. When have we sinful humans, even after we get saved, done a really good job of being "righteous by impulse?" Paul, after getting saved, said, "I know that in me, that is in my flesh, dwelleth no good thing."

Money is an every single day thing, and thus God had a lot to say about it. War was an every now and then thing, so

252

He had much less to say about it. Giving birth was an every now and then thing, so He had much less to say about it. It simply makes sense that, since money is an everyday thing, we would find a lot about it both in Old and New Testaments, and we do.

But at no time do we ever find anything that should cause us to call the character of God into question. In fact, the most careful person ever on the subject was Jesus Himself. Do you remember that coin that was a ransom for the soul? It became an issue for Him one day:

Matthew 17:24 *And when they were come to Capernaum, they that received tribute money came to Peter, and said, Doth not your master pay tribute?* **25** *He saith, Yes. And when he was come into the house, Jesus prevented him, saying, What thinkest thou, Simon? of whom do the kings of the earth take custom or tribute? of their own children, or of strangers?* **26** *Peter saith unto him, Of strangers. Jesus saith unto him, Then are the children free.* **27** *Notwithstanding, lest we should offend them, go thou to the sea, and cast an hook, and take up the fish that first cometh up; and when thou hast opened his mouth, thou shalt find a piece of money: that take, and give unto them for me and thee.*

Jesus Himself gave that coin. The very Son of God was incredibly careful to live just as He had commanded others in Scripture, even though He was the one that did not need it.

Works Cited

Ammi, Ken, "Dan Barker – His Views on Human Dignity." www.truefreethinker.com/articles/dan-barker-his-views-human-dignity Accessed 2/9/2018

Aquinas, Thomas, *Summa Theologica.* 2a, Question 99, Article 4

Barker, Dan, "For Goodness Sake.: (https://ffrf.org/legacy/about/bybarker/goodness.php)

Barker, Dan, *Godless.* Ulysse, 2008

British Family Bible Notes, Power Bible CD software, 2001

Clarke, Adam, *Clarke's Commentary.* Abingdon-Cokesbury Press, 6 vols.

Dawkins, Richard, *The God Delusion.* (https://www.goodreads.com/quotes/23651) Accessed 1/20/2018

Debate between Dan Barker and Peter Payne at the University of Wisconsin." March 14, 2005, 35:10 as quoted on https://carm.org/list-quotes-dan-barker

Harris, Sam, *The End of Faith.* Norton, 2005

Henry, Matthew, *Commentary on the Whole Bible*, Fleming H. Revell Company. 6 vols.

Hentoff, Nat, "A Professor of Infanticide at Princeton." (http://www.jewishworldreview.com/cols/hentoff0913 99.asp) Accessed 2/8/2018

Horowitz, Ami, "Berkeley students' surprising reaction to ISIS and Israel flags on campus." 11/19/2014 (http://www.foxnews.com/opinion/2014/11/19/berkeley-students-surprising-reaction-to-isis-and-israeli-flags-on-campus.html)

Howell, Kellan, "Saida Grundy, Boston University Professor: White males a 'Problem Population.' " May 9, 2015 (https://www.washingtontimes.com/news/2015/may/9/saida-grundy-boston-university-professor-white-mal)

https://www.kenyatalk.com/index.php?threads/gods-12-biggest-d-ck-moves-in-the-old-testament.22273 Accessed 2/8/2018

International Standard Bible Encyclopaedia. WM. B. Eerdmans, 1952. 6 vols.

Jamieson, Robert, et al., *A Commentary on the Old and New Testaments.* Hendrickson, 4th ed., 2008, 3 vols.

Nielsen, Robert, "Terrible Parts of the Bible: Part 5 – Racism" 5/3/2012 (https://whistlinginthewind.org/2012/05/03/terrible-parts-of-the-bible-part-5-racism)

Rachels, James *Created from Animals: The Moral Implications of Darwinism.* Oxford, 1990

Richardson, Sheri Ann, "Vegetables That Don't Grow Well Together" (https://www.gardenguides.com/101917-vegetables-dont-grow-well-together.html.) Accessed 2/8/2018

Roth, Kenneth, "Despots Pretending to Spot and Shame Despots." Human Rights Watch. 4/17/2001

(https://www.hrw.org/news/2001/04/17/despots-pretending-spot-and-shame-despots)

Salstrand, George A. E., *The Tithe.* Baker Book House, 1952

Singer, Peter, *Pediatrics.* Vol 72, No. 1, July 1983, p 129

Specter, Michael, *New Yorker,* "The Dangerous Philosopher." 9/6/1999 (https://www.newyorker.com/magazine/1999/09/06/the-dangerous-philosopher)

Webster, Daniel, (https://www.goodreads.com/quotes/45253-if-religious-books-are-not-widely-circulated-among-the-masses) Accessed 2/8/2018

Wiesel, Elie, *Night.* Hill and Wang, Translated Marion Wiesel, 2006

Willmington, H. L., *Willmington's Guide to the Bible.* Tyndale, 1986, 2 vols.

www.historyembalmed.org/ancient-egyptians/egyptian-women.htm

www.nrlc.org/archive/news/1999/NRL999/pres.html Accessed 2/8/2018

Zacharias, Ravi, "Why suffering: The Question." (www.http://rzim.org/just-thinking/why-suffering-the-question) Accessed 2/8/2018

Other Books by Dr. Bo Wagner

From Footers to Finish Nails
Beyond the Colored Coat
Marriage Makers, Marriage Breakers
Daniel: Breathtaking
Esther: Five Feast and the Finger Prints of God
Nehemiah: A Labor of Love
Romans: Salvation From A-Z
Ruth: Diamonds in the Darkness
Don't Muzzle the Ox
I'm Saved! Now What???

Fiction Titles

The Night Heroes Series:

Cry From the Coal Mine (Vol. 1)
Free Fall (Vol. 2)
Broken Brotherhood (Vol. 3)
The Blade of Black Crow (Vol. 4)
Ghost Ship (Vol. 5)
When Serpents Rise (Vol. 6)
Moth Man (Vol. 7)

Sci-Fi

Zak Blue and the Great Space Chase:

Falcon Wing (Vol. 1)

Made in the USA
Columbia, SC
01 March 2018